New Song of God's Grace Embraced

Josephine Sealy

TEACH Services, Inc.
PUBLISHING
www.TEACHServices.com • (800) 367-1844

World rights reserved. This book or any portion thereof may not be copied or reproduced in any form or manner whatever, except as provided by law, without the written permission of the publisher, except by a reviewer who may quote brief passages in a review.

The author assumes full responsibility for the accuracy of all facts and quotations as cited in this book. The opinions expressed in this book are the author's personal views and interpretations, and do not necessarily reflect those of the publisher.

This book is provided with the understanding that the publisher is not engaged in giving spiritual, legal, medical, or other professional advice. If authoritative advice is needed, the reader should seek the counsel of a competent professional.

Copyright © 2019 Josephine Sealy

Copyright © 2019 TEACH Services, Inc.

ISBN-13: 978-1-4796-1047-1 (Paperback)

ISBN-13: 978-1-4796-1048-8 (ePub)

Library of Congress Control Number: 2019938487

Published by

Table of Contents

Introduction 9
Acknowledgments 11
What Others Have Said 12
God's Gift to Us 13
Come, Share the Joy of Poetry 14
God Has So Many Gifts 15
Be Happy for God's Blessings 16
Appreciate Your Blessings, Large or Small 17
Give Me All of the Above 17
Man Creating? 18
My Lord, You Know 19

The Wonder, Power, and Beauty of Nature 21
Delightful Days, versus Dreary Days 22
Glory Outshines Beauty 23
You Cannot Stop the Storm 25
The Wind, the Window, and the Housewife 26
Springtime! 27
Standing Firm 28
Light Overpowers Darkness 29
Strength and Power of the Deep 29
Can Anything Hide from the Sun? 30
Complex World 31
Time 32
Taking to Give 33
A Lesson from My Maple Tree 34
Good Morning, Little Bird 35
Resting in the Son, After Racing with the Sun 36
Gloom Chasers 37
The Hummingbird *(A Childhood Memory)* 38
Fireflies *(A Childhood Memory)* 39
Worms and Butterflies *(A Childhood Memory)* 40
Coconut Palm *(A Childhood and Young Adult Memory)* 41
What Seeds Can Do *(A Childhood and Young Adult Memory)* 42
God's Brilliant Wonder Ink 43

Repentance and Transformation 47
This Is What the Child of God Must Do 48
The Voice of Conscience 49
Depression Breaker 49
Bid Them Depart 49
Plea for Comfort and Escape 50
Men's Laws versus God's Compassion 50
God's Transforming Power 51
Longing for Renewal 51
Repentance 52
Lord Put Enmity 53
Train My Mind, O Lord 53
We Need True Repentance 54
Right about Face 56
Saul, Changed to Paul 57
Reflections 58
May I Likewise Live 59
Help Me to Be Ready 60
Sealed Forever 61

Christ's Return and Salvation 63
Praises to Our Coming King 64
No More Sinkholes 65
We Will Be Going to God's House 67
Heaven's Invitation 68
Oh, When? 68
Waiting Saints 69
Wise Choice Abraham Made 69
Transient versus Permanent Structures 71
Wake Up! The King Is Coming! 72
We Shall Come with Gladness 73
Always a Servant 74
Christ Will Make Sure 75
Accept God's Offers 76
Heavenly Train 77
Earthly Problems Light and Gone 78
This Earth Neither Safe nor Permanent 79
God Shall Make Our Bodies Anew 80
They Shall Behold His Glory 82

God's Strength and Guidance 83
Walking with Jesus 84
Early Let Me Rise... 84
Who Am I Really Serving on the Job? 84
God Has Something to Say Every Day 85
Lift Me and Guide Me 85
Oh, How Can We Serve? 86
Jesus, Our Dear Savior 87
Out of a Hard Day 87
God Woos Us in the Morning 88
Recognizing and Trusting Christ 88
Do We Really Know? 89
Let All Heaven Now Rejoice 91
Trust God Always 92
Prayer for Rest.. 92
May We Escape Sin's Entrapment 93
My Best Friend 94

Friendship and Family Matters................................ 95
To My Sister Ethel.. 96
Prayer for Air Travel Safety 97
When Facing Threat or Harm 97
Prayer for Safety Away from Home 98
Teach Us How to Love 99
Morning Exercise Booster 100
Waiting for You 101
Reciprocated Love 101
God's Commands versus Satan's Lies............................. 102
Why Did God Make Woman and Man? 105
Infants' Pleas and Moms' Resolve................................ 106
Wives, Wives, Be Alive! 107
Money Flies 108
The Ruins of Gossip 109
Tolerate the Children 110
Never Woman Without Man 110
Jesus Also Cares 111
May It Go Well 113
Children Like to Play 115
Mothers, Be Alert! 116

God's Uniqueness 117
Love Song 118
God Makes Wonderful Things. 119
God's Love Seen in What He Has Made 120
God Is, and Will Always Be Alive 121
Miracle Divine. 121
God Alone Is Love 122
God Hears and Understands Our Prayers 123
God Is a Good God. 124
God Loves the Handicapped 125
God Has Made All Things for Good. 126
God's Touch. 127
Spiritual Food Is the Best. 127
God Made Various Things from the Same Soil 129
Jesus' Name Lives On. 130
God Does Great Things 130
Nebuchadnezzar's Dream 131
God's Sunshine and Rain. 132
God's Life-Sustaining Air. 133
Why I Believe in God 134
Great God Who Lives Forever 135
God's Wisdom Bank. 136

Coping with Death 139
Sorrowful Lament with Hope 140
Peace and Resurrection 141
Death Will Be Sweet Sleep. 142
I Will See God's Lovely Face 143
My Sister Rose Ann 144

Trusting God's Ability to Help and Save 145
By God Who Is Creator 146
Our Worst Enemy 146
I'll Praise God Whatever 147
Let Me Bless the Lord 147
God Sent Light, Joy, and Peace. 149
The Mighty Tug of War. 150
Christ's Victory over Satan. 151
Gratitude 152
Leave the Cleansing to God. 153
Riding on God's Train. 154

It's Meant to Make You Glad 155
We Wrestle Against Evil......................................156
In Thee I Hope 157
Faith and Hope 158
Turn Aside from Suicide......................................159
Battle for Bread?..160
Survival..161
Kind versus Unkind Employers................................162
God Will Sustain 163
Cold Chasing Song and Prayer 165

Experiencing God's Love 167
Morning Wish 168
Glad and Grateful...168
What We Need Most...169
Teach Us How to Love 169
God Loves You 170

Salvation Through Christ and Other Vital Truths 171
Figurative Mountain...172
Christ Is Our Righteousness.................................173
Listen World—God's Love Song to You.........................174
Whom Shall I Choose?..176
Followed..177
The Perfect Pastor..178
Be on Guard, Watchmen 179
Sensible versus Silly Soldiers 180
The Bell with the Clapper 181
God's Clocks 183
Peace When? and Where?......................................184
God's Truth Will Triumph 185
Oh, Jesus, Oh...186
God's Forgiveness...187

What God Requires of Us......................................189
Glory to My King 190
Focusing on God...191
Your Body Is My Temple 192
Jesus, Shine Your Light on Me 193
I Worship the God of Heaven 193
Read the Bible, Friends 194
Disbelief and Disobedience..................................196

Blow the Trumpet, Watchman 198
Abiding in Christ...199
Mutual Concern 200
To Share with Love 201
Beware, Beware..204
Timothy 204
God, the Center of Church and Home 205
Noah and the Animals Obeyed 206
I Want to Be like Jesus Most of All.............................208

Each poem is accompanied by a Bible reference. These are the texts that inspired the author to create the poem. Feel free to explore the Scriptures so that you too, may be inspired by the Word of God.

Introduction

Dear Reader,

I hope you will enjoy the poems which you are about to read in this book, and not only enjoy but consider them seriously since some of them may go against the grain of what you might currently believe. These poems all relate to everyday life experiences. They are not meant to stir up controversies, but as a fellow traveler in this world, I feel a need to draw your attention to certain issues which you may not have considered.

Ever since childhood, my environment has been saturated with poetry, religious songs, nursery rhymes, poetry reading, and poetry memorization. I like using the literary form of poetry because I am able to better express and share my thoughts with others through the use of its concise format of lines and rhymes. Although environmental factors influence the construction of my poems, I strongly believe my ability to write them is God-given, and that they are meant to be shared an enjoyed by people everywhere.

When I moved to Michigan in the early 1970s, I began to write poetry often. Those poems as well as those written from 2005, when I moved to Florida, emerged out of things which I observed or experienced. Having a family to care for, and sometimes the responsibility of a full time job, I could not always pen my thoughts at the moment they came to me, so I would quickly write them in code, and wait for a later opportunity when I could sit down and write them out fully.

Frequently, I would forget parts of my poems, so I often resorted to prayer, asking God to bring them back to my memory, and God would answer. The words would come flowing, and many times the poems would be better than how I first perceived them. Even now, when a poetic thought comes to mind, I pray about it: "Heavenly Father, I have this idea. I know what I want to say, but I do not know how to say it. Please help me with this poem," and God always comes to my rescue; so glory be to His name! I could not have done it without Him.

My favorite poets are writers of sacred songs and verses; those who give glory to God, who extol His majesty, power, and grace, who talk of His love, mercy, compassion, forgiveness, and the joy and peace He bestows on those who seek and believe in Him. Because of the nature of man, and the sinful condition of the world in general, we need encouragement, direction, and instruction.

We need to know that God is ever present. In spite of the dismal state of our world and the chaos which surrounds us. We need to know there is hope that we are not alone, that we will be delivered, and there is light for those who stumble in the dark. Writers of sacred poetry and verses give such encouragement.

Those who suffer in various ways but believe in God and accept His grace can find hope, solace, and comfort when soothed by sacred poems. The poetic writings found in the books of Psalms, Proverbs, Ecclesiastes, and elsewhere in the Bible, give good guidance and encouragement to all who read them and acknowledge the Author, God, as the source of its inspiration. Through the reading of sacred verses contained in the Holy Bible, I found myself a sinner in need of God's grace. I repented of my sins and embraced God's grace. I hope you do the same as you move from this book to the words of God contained in the Bible, which I strongly recommend you read. You will notice that each poem is accompanied by a Bible reference. These are the texts that inspired the author to create that poem and they can help you as you begin your journey of delving into the wonderful truths of God's Word.

"For the grace of God that bringeth salvation hath appeared to all men, Teaching us that, denying ungodliness and worldly lusts, we should live soberly, righteously, and godly, in this present world; Looking for the blessed hope, and the glorious appearing of the great God and our Saviour Jesus Christ; Who gave Himself for us, that He might redeem us from all iniquity ... That being justified by His grace, we should be made heirs according to the hope of eternal life." Titus 2:11–14; 3:7. May God bless you; and happy reading!

Acknowledgments

Thanks to God, my heavenly Father, and Sustainer, for enabling me to write poetry. Could not have done it without His help and enabling power.

Also want to thank my children, Vernetta Sealy and Vernol Sealy Jr. for helping me immensely, with the technological aspects of getting this book done.

Thanks to Jim and Carolyn Sutton, Carle Ephraim, and Adventist World Radio's prayer team, for giving their support in prayer, when called upon to pray that this book would become a reality, or when I needed to meet the deadlines of the publisher.

Thanks to my friend, Maylyn Benjamin Ambrose, through whom I obtained my first overseas job. That experience became a catalyst of many challenges which have led me to a closer walk of faith and trust in God.

Many thanks for the patience and support of Teach Services, in getting this book done.

What Others Have Said

"I feel that when each poem is read, it inspires one to draw closer to the Lord. The book really embraces the Holy Scriptures with a unique style of poetry that shows the creative mind of the author. This is a great book for all to read and add to their library"
—Dorothy Robinson, Retired Clerk, Children's Story Time organizer, Head Deaconess, and Personal Ministries Secretary

"These poems give the reader the impression that they have been penned by someone who has a close walk with the Lord. Though the author acknowledges earthly realities such as pain and loss, she points the reader to Jesus, whose sovereign plans offer hope eternal."
—James and Carolyn Sutton, AWR Ambassador, Radio Bible Program Co-host, and Local Church Elder (James); AWR Ambassador, Former Missionary to Africa, Retired Editor and Teacher (Carolyn)

"The work of art: *New Song of God's Grace Embraced* by Josephine Sealy. I highly recommend the printing and reading of the poetry of Mrs. Josephine Sealy. This collection is a God-given source of encouragement to the church and the world. It is a work well done! These sobering poems are needed in a world that is in deep despair and a sea of trouble. This high-profile work of art in poetry is worthy to grace every home around the world. Adults and children alike can read this collection of poetry.
"The author is a homemaker and a dedicated Christian mother of two (Vernol and Vernetta Sealy). She is highly dedicated in her daily witness for Jesus through sharing time with others around her. Mrs. Sealy has many hobbies, such as gardening, cooking, and her special drink "sorrel" with a flavor that cannot be beat! It is a high honor to endorse the printing of her book and sprit-filled writings, which should be presented to the world. Godspeed and blessings!"
—Joseph P. Lewis, Retired Pastor, Emeritus, South Western Union Conference

Joseph P. Lewis, II
Kathleen T. Lewis

God's Gift to Us

Come, Share the Joy of Poetry
Matthew 5:14

Poetry is that good seed God puts within my soul.
That precious little fertile seed that's worth more to me than gold.

And when God gently placed it there, He meant that it should grow;
And then to blossom everywhere, wherever I may go.

And it is as the Scripture says, "All things will come to light."
Gifts better on a "candlestick," Than hid 'neath shades of night.

And we can say that secret love was never meant to be.
True love is more enduring when it's open, pure, and free.

And what's the use of making songs, never meant to be heard.
Might as well then, freeze the ocean, or stop a flying bird.

Since all God's gifts are given to be shared and to be used,
Come share the joy of poetry. Embrace them if you choose.

But God alone deserves the praise who gives us bounteous gifts always.
And may the gifts so freely given, always point to God and heaven.

God Has So Many Gifts
1 Corinthians 13:13

God has so many gifts to share,
You can ask Him if you care.

Some may ask for earthly wealth,
Others ask for perfect health.

"Faith, and hope, and charity,"
These He gives us all for free.

I was asking Him for much,
But He only gave me such,

That He knew that I could use.
Such I accept, and not refuse.

Be Happy for God's Blessings
Psalm 68:19

Be happy for the sunshine, and be happy for the breeze.
Be happy for the green grass, and be happy for the trees.

Be happy for the transient clouds that pass so slowly by.
Be happy for the winged birds gliding through the sky.

Be happy for the waters which man and beast can drink.
Be happy for your ears that hear and for your eyes that blink.

Be happy for your hands, and be happy for your feet.
Be happy for your talking tongues and for your hearts that beat.

Be happy for the luscious fruits which you and I can eat.
Be happy for those vegetables, spicy, mild, or sweet.

Since all the good things God has made, are too numerous to count,
Let's just be happy for them all, concluding with a shout.

Praise the Lord! Praise the Lord! Praise the Lord!

Appreciate Your Blessings, Large or Small
Romans 12:6

When God distributes blessings,
Some receive a small amount.
And then again to some He gives,
More than they can count.

He knows what we can manage;
What with our share we'll do;
So let's give thanks for what He gave,
Be it many, or but few.

Give Me All of the Above
Matthew 7:7–8

What is my priority?
Life, love, peace, longevity?
This is not so hard to solve.
Give me all of the above.

Man Creating?
Genesis 1–2:7

I view with awe and wonder,
The creative things men do.
How does this creativity
Of man appear to you?

I think that when God made man
And gave him gifts galore,
He included creativity for him,
So he would not be a bore.

He made man's mind with visions
Of things moving all around,
And not with bland opinions
Of things fastened to the ground.

And just how man accomplished it,
Is something to behold.
Yea, God gave man good wits,
And not brains stern and cold.

So man, not for one moment
Become too vain and proud,
That you cannot acknowledge
That your wits come from the Lord.

My Lord, You Know
Matthew 25:14–29

My Lord, I know that You know,
Just why I like to write.
I am not thinking rivalry,
Or to put on a grand show.

You know that I just want to use
The gifts you've given to me.
To answer "yes," when You'll
Demand accountability.

I want not, at Your coming,
To hang my head in shame.
I hope that You've not given me,
Your precious gifts in vain.

I want not to return to You
Your precious gifts the same.
You intended they would multiply
To be given to You with gain.

So may You bless the precious gifts
That You have given to me,
That they may do a world of good,
To Your children, and to Thee.

20

The Wonder, Power, and Beauty of Nature

Delightful Days, versus Dreary Days
Psalm 50:15

When the days are sunny and bright,
We go zipping along, we are filled with delight.
We are joyous and happy as we journey along;
Sometimes even humming or singing a song.

The scenes are inviting, the skies clear and blue.
And we watch white clouds sailing along, too.
We are conscious of travelers passing us by.
Are they having a good day? That they may not deny.

But when days are dreary, and skies become grey,
And all around seems filled with dismay;
We try to be careful and keep in our lanes.
The slightest mistake could result in our pain.

The roads could be icy or covered with snow.
And through rising water we know we can't go.
The rain could be falling in torrents, too.
We are praying to God that we'll safely get through.

This is also the way with our real life.
We are all very happy when life's a delight.
Yes, we feel such joy and contentment within,
As we are blessed by our Maker, and loved by our kin.

But, when life takes a bad turn—oh, what can we do?
Since we know that God cares, and can rescue us, too.
We beseech Him to deliver us from our present plight,
And He answers our prayers, with much joy and delight.

Glory Outshines Beauty
Malachi 4:2

Beholding sun in cloudless sky is sure a scene of glory,
The rising or the setting sun is yet another story.
Sun, when attended by the clouds, creates a scene of beauty.
I saw one rising billowing cloud, it did not seem appealing.
Not coupled with the rising sun, 'twas not at all exciting.
I was pondering days before how sun and clouds make beauty.
Clouds without sun in our lives does make it dark and dreary.

When life's clouds break up and light appears, we are very happy.
God never lets our life's dark clouds stay, or go on forever.
Like lonely cloud in yonder sky which gained a golden lining;
When faithful sun with steady speed the cloud was overtaking.
Lonely cloud became transformed, by sun's overwhelming glory.
It was no more looking then, somber, dark, and dreary.
The sun gained pace above the cloud, then all was only glory.

Now where's that cloud, which for a while had a golden lining?
Sun's glory which o'ertook the cloud just sent it into hiding.
And I am hoping that my God will quell my earthly strife,
And banish clouds of failure, and of sin, from my tattered life.
I hope that soon, and very soon, delivering light will come.
It may not be, or will not be, 'til Christ shall take me home.
But I will wait, patiently wait, and I will keep the faith,
Until I see the glorious light, beaming from heaven's gate.

You Cannot Stop the Storm
Psalm 135:5–7

You cannot stop the lightning,
And you cannot stop the rain.
You cannot stop the thunder
From sounding again.

You cannot stop the waves,
And you cannot stop the breeze.
You cannot stop the floods
That run into the seas.

But you can seek shelter
And get out of the way,
When these awesome forces,
Their Creator obey.

You cannot stop the storm,
So it is best to pray
To God for some safety,
As storms go on their way.

The Wind, the Window, and the Housewife
Song of Solomon 2:11–13

Open, little window.
I must get some breeze.
I am starved for fresh air.
Open, if you please.

I cannot freely open,
As you ask of me.
I am fixed and armless,
Just as you can see.

She opened up the window
And waited for fresh air
To caress her nostrils,
Her neck, her face, her hair.

Steady, little window.
I am coming through.
You've kept me out all winter,
But now I'll blow through you.

This is so refreshing.
I like this gentle breeze.
You can keep on coming.
Blow on, if you please.

Springtime!
Isaiah 35:1

Oh the joy of springtime,
When all the flowering trees
Begin to blossom and to bud
Before they bring forth leaves.

They seem to make the spirits soar,
And, oh, what joy they bring.
Beholding them through pane or door
Just makes me want to sing.

Cherry trees dressed up like brides;
Crab apples join the show.
And all my garden flowers take pride
To wave, and toss, and glow.

That's why I like to water them,
And pull the bad weeds out.
And afterwards, surveying them,
I feel that I could shout.

Thank God for flowering trees.
They mend my spirits so.
And in my pleasant garden lees
All spring, I hope to go.

'Till summer comes, and fall impends,
And sparkling snowflakes fall,
I'll cherish all the things God sends
To cheer and bless us all.

Lord, help us to enjoy the trees
And flowers You give to us;
But let us learn to love You more,
And in Your wisdom trust.

Standing Firm
Joshua 1:9

I watched this flower on a bright summer day,
As the wind tried hard to blow it away.

Sure from time to time the flower would duck,
But she stood her ground, and never gave up.

You could see from her pose that she had a good knack,
As how to resist, and how to bounce back.

The wind could not shake the flower a bit,
So finally defeated, he just had to quit,

And retreated back to his hiding place;
But the flower was left with a smile on her face.

And that is how trials will try to shake us.
But we shall survive if in God we trust.

May God give us the strength, and also the grace,
To put the devil in his place.

And just like the strength that flower displayed,
May we be strong and unafraid.

With Christ on our side, courageous we'll be,
And through His strength, win the victory.

Light Overpowers Darkness
Psalm 97:11

Wow! The light came in.
Where did the darkness go?
When the sun shines in,
It turns the dark to light.

And when you flip the light switch,
That also makes it bright.
Isn't that amazing? Seems a miracle to me.
The dark not only disappears,
But I can clearly see.

God is waiting to rid darkness from our souls.
If we let God have His way with us,
'Twill be light with His control.

Strength and Power of the Deep
Psalm 107:23–32

I do not trifle with the ocean.
It is too vast, and deep, and strong.
Nor will I trifle with the sea.
It is too powerful for me.

Some who hearkened to their lure,
Have not returned safely to shore.
So cautious I will always be,
With the great ocean and the sea.

Can Anything Hide from the Sun?
Psalm 19:4–6

I am always so amazed, to see how that bright sun works.
Just as the Bible says, it warms everything on earth.
Have you ever noticed at a certain time of year,
That in one corner of your house, you see the sunshine there;
Then later in the year, from that spot it slowly disappears?

But in another corner, the sun begins to glow.
And so I watch with wonder. Wow! God hath made it so.
I used to move the plants around, but now I let that go.
I sensed that God had made a plan to make my house plants grow.

I also came to learn that sunshine, household germs can kill.
And so I let the sunshine sanitize the house at will.
Sometimes we take for granted, what God's creations do.
But if you stop to ponder them, they're God's great love for you.

Complex World
Isaiah 55:10–11

The world is flat. The world is round.
The world is square. It spins around.

What else about the world is known?
It also travels up, and down.

Encompassed by the deep blue sea,
And wind that's blowing constantly.

It's blessed with water from above,
And guided by the God of love.

Shrouded by such complexity,
Its wonders are too great for me.

Time

Exodus 20:8–11

Time: complicated thing it is.
Time flies. It runs. It crawls. It leaps
And seems the hardest thing to keep.

Yes, time can creep, then slips away,
Though it belongs to night and day.
It's working time, then resting time.
It also turns to hallowed time.

It marches on, then steals away,
And then returns another day.
Though we do right, or we do wrong,
It seems that time goes on and on.

But we should do right every hour,
For soon there will be time no more.

Taking to Give
Matthew 14:17–20

Big, white, fluffy clouds loom over the Gulf,
Drawing up water; later dumping it on land.
And so abundant waters flow,
Watering plants to make them grow.

Quenching the thirst of man and beast,
Producing food so they can feast.
And the Atlantic does the same.
They give glory to God's name,

Who makes the sea, the clouds, the rain?
And all the seas the world around,
Do share their water with the clouds,
That ever to the earth draw nigh,

To share their water from the sky.
If like the clouds, we take to give
The good which God forever gives,
We'll bless the world in which we live.

A Lesson from My Maple Tree
Matthew 18:20

I saw within my garden, a very tiny tree.
It had not many leaves, only two or three.
Its frailty seemed to crave any mercy I could give,
So I considered for a while if I should make it live.

I reasoned then unto myself, 'twas God who placed it there;
That since He made it grow, then my garden it could share.
And so I left the little twig and watched it as it grew.
It did so well as it enjoyed the sun, the rain, the dew.

In time that very little plant became a stately tree,
And through my bedroom window, it was staring in at me.
It seemed so very happy as it waved in passing breeze;
And happier it seemed to me than all the other trees.

It seemed as if triumphant over what it left below,
That it could freely reach above and toward heaven go;
For now instead of hugging dirt, its background is the sky,
And now it is a haven for most creatures passing by.

Nimble little squirrels find some rest in its cool shade.
And tiny little birds reside in nests that they have made.
And I for one am glad for shade upon my window pane;
And for cool breeze it sends my way time and time again.

There is a goodly lesson in that God-sent maple tree.
I hope You can consider it and see just what I see.
We can leave the world's muck below and rise above its din;
As heavenward we soar to God and rise above our sin.

Good Morning, Little Bird
Song of Solomon 2:12

Good morning, little bird.
Though you are not near me,
Your sweet voice I heard.
Are you standing on a tree?
Or on a lowly thistle
With your vibrant whistle?

And though it is not long,
I love that melodious song.
But how soon you fly away,
To roam and forage for the day.
Please, do come my way again
With your melodious strain.

Resting in the Son, After Racing with the Sun
John 14:1–3

When the sun gets up by day, it doesn't stop to query.
Its face is bright. It wears no frown and does not even worry.
It rises up with warmth and glow, and you can see it's strong.
And he appears to "run a race," while winning all day long.

Well, people often say they "try to beat the clock."
And so they try with all their might to work, and never slack.
But I think what they are really doing, is, trying to beat the sun.
But that great big fireball, always men outrun.

And so men, tired, would go to sleep; then try another day,
But the sun never sleeps at all, but runs while humans lay.
It is such good fun though, to try to beat the sun.
And though we often lose the race, it helps us get things done.

We appreciate its blessings. It shares with us its light.
As it lingers, we're more cheery, and it always makes things bright.
We should appreciate it more. Its warmth causes things to grow.
And this should keep us humble: it's above, we are below.

Now, let us turn our thoughts, much higher, to God's dear Son.
We know that "He arises with healing in His wings."
More than our transient sun, God's Son brings warmth and love.
And He'll be coming back, to take us to His home above.

We know a day is coming when the sun with its bright light,
Will be there no more to serve us. It will vanish from our sight.
For all the light we'll ever need, will be the Lord alone.
As we all gather to worship, and sing praises 'round His throne.

Then forever, through the Son of God, we'll truly find sweet rest.
Along with all the other blessings, God will shower on the blessed.

Gloom Chasers
Isaiah 35:4

What brilliant colors on the trees!
What verdant pastures in the lees!
And billowing clouds that race on by
Suspended in an azure sky.

No gloominess, but sunshine bright,
Has made this day a sheer delight.
And these delights make people say,
"This lifts the spirit, cheers the day."

It makes each wear a smiling face,
As if one feels a warm embrace.
It fills the heart with hope and peace.
Oh, that such joys would never cease.

But days are never always bright.
Sometimes the clouds shut out the light.
Or sunset that is meant for rest
Bring shades of gray or sheer darkness.

But one while resting through the night,
Can dream of morn's returning light.
And so it is with life I'd say,
God's delights can chase our gloom away.

The Hummingbird
(A Childhood Memory)
Psalm 50:11

The hummingbird seems but a very small thing,
With long slender beak and very small wings.
It seems not to rest. It's as busy as can be.
Its movement is swift and enchanting, but free.

I like to watch it as it dives for a flower,
And dines on sweet nectar hour by hour.
I follow its flight as far as I can see.
To it none compares, but the wise honeybee.

And though it is fragile, and sings not a song,
It seems to be joyfully darting along.
And I think that of all the small flying birds,
None can compare to that fine hummingbird.

Fireflies
(A Childhood Memory)
John 1:5

Fireflies, fireflies flying all around.
They are on the trees and on the ground.
They are flying low. They are flying high.
They look like stars that are up in the sky.

They are such a pretty sight to see,
On any dark night, on a roof or a tree.
Fireflies, fireflies flying so high.
They look like lights as they pass us by.

They are all so luminous and bright.
To us they are such a welcome sight.
When comes the night and gone the day,
We love to chase the fireflies and play.

Sometimes we children catch the fireflies,
Just to see what their bodies look like.
And we would find that on our clothes,
Their amber light just glows and glows.

Fireflies, fireflies flying everywhere.
We see their lights, but no sound we hear.
Oh how we love those roaming fireflies;
Darting and shining like stars in the sky.

Worms and Butterflies
(A Childhood Memory)
Ecclesiastes 3:1

See the caterpillar and the inchworm?
I do not like how they squirm.
But my little sister does not mind at all.
She likes them, and she plays with them all.

They tumble and crawl on branches of trees
And then they devour the juicy green leaves
Some have pretty stripes on their bodies and backs
They come in bright colors, green, yellow, and black.

They eat and they eat, their small stomachs to fill;
Then they will lie down, and rest very still.
Soon they cover themselves with a silky cocoon.
Then sleep in the morning, at night, and at noon.

They are transforming. They are no more worms.
They cease to tumble, and stretch, and squirm.
If they are not worms, then what can they be?
We should not disturb them; but let's wait and see.

My mom says they are resting, and by and by,
They will be turned into bright butterflies.
And that was the truth, for one day by and by,
Out from the cocoons came bright butterflies.

Coconut Palm
(A Childhood and Young Adult Memory)
Psalm 1:1–3

Coconut palm, coconut palm;
Down in the land where it's sunny and warm.
It bows in the breeze and writhes in the storm.
Oh, how I love the coconut palm.

The coconut palm is a useful plant.
It gives you most any comfort you want.
It can give you food or refreshing drink.
Provides shade while you stop and think.

From its leaves a basket you can make,
To carry fish that are yours for the take.
Its leaves will also make walls and roofs.
You can lie within it, as you read a book.

When the fruit of that palm is sturdy but green,
Everyone loves to drink its cool drink, so it seems.
Now carefully cut that green coconut,
And have a sweet drink, from its very own cup.

When strong boys climb up the coconut tree,
All the children there, are as happy as can be.
For whether the fruits are green or they're dry.
They provide goodies—drinks, candies, or pies.

From the coconut palm, you can also plait,
A shopping bag, or a fancy broad hat.
You can make a mat to lay on the ground,
While all your relatives gather around.

Dear coconut palm, how I do miss you.
Down in the land where it's sunny and blue.
There you wave in the breeze, bow and twist, too.
And I'm sure everyone in the tropics loves you.

What Seeds Can Do
(A Childhood and Young Adult Memory)
James 3:18

Seeds of brown and gray and black,
Can make many things, can brighten a sack.
Some seeds are pretty, multicolored at that.
Use them for beads, or to decorate a hat.

Sometimes you can play a game with seeds,
When you are tired turning them into beads.
Take for instance, the smooth round wari.
It's the size of a marble, as you can see.

It is gray or orange, but never black.
Throw it or toss it. It will never crack.
It grows on a tree. It costs not a dime.
And it can be kept for a very long time.

There is also that black, round bona seed.
It comes from a tree, not just from a weed.
Under a shady tree or in the bright sun,
You can use it as a marble for more fun.

Seeds can also grow, as you well know.
It is the very reason that we plant and sow.
The seeds that we get from peaches or peas,
Will bring us fruits in the upcoming years.

Some seeds can be turned into pleasant food.
Sweet corn or peanuts can taste very good.
Seeds can feed the birds and the animals, too.
They are very useful. I like them, don't you?

God's Brilliant Wonder Ink
Psalm 113:3

Oh, how glorious is the sunrise!
How it brightens up the sky!
It brings joy to all God's creatures;
Joy to every seeing eye.
The sun peeks over the mountain,
Sending sunbeams gleaming down.
They're so bright they make you blink.
And it seems that they are painted
With God's brilliant wonder ink.

And the beauty of the rainbow,
God's designs of color reveal.
Such beauty in that mercy arc,
That to every heart appeals.
With its cheery brilliant colors,
Happiness it makes you feel.
Oh, what beauty God included,
In that glorious semi wheel!
It's a teacher to true artists.
It's a masterpiece, I think.
And I know it's also painted,
With God's brilliant wonder ink.

They say the stars up in the sky,
Are very glorious too.
Each one reflects rare beauty.
Each one wears a different hue.
I have never seen them close up,
But someday I hope I can.
I guess that I would be so thrilled
As with joy I view each one.
And I know that there must be
A power that makes them blink;
And an all-wise Being
Who makes them glow
With His brilliant wonder ink.

Even autumn leaves seem painted
With many different colors.
Though they may last for just
A while, or hours upon hours.
Who can deny such scenes bring
Cheer to all, each passing year?
They are treasured up in pictures,
So that their memories would last.
We look forward to their beauty,
And we think about their past.

Though their frail lives are short,
Yet, none could deny, I think,
That these are also painted,
With God's brilliant wonder ink.
And whether beautiful flowers grow
By choice, or wild beside the way,
God's love and care and wisdom,
They instantly display.

Wherever they are scattered,
They always bring good cheer,
To the weak and to the strong,
And sick folks everywhere.
They have such welcome colors.
They are yellow, purple, green, red,
White, blue, orange, or bright pink.
And whatever is the color,
It's God's brilliant wonder ink.

And many little creatures,
And sometimes big ones, too
Are painted with bright colors.
We can see them in the zoo.
And seashells, rocks, and timber,
All have a special hue.
And minerals that glitter,
Wear some favorite colors, too.
And if you care to look around,
There are things that you could find

That are filled with cheerful colors.
All these natural things, I think,
Are bountifully painted
With God's brilliant wonder ink.

The color of your hair, your nails,
And the color of your eyes,
Are all a part of God's great thought,
For He is sure all-wise.
He fashioned you with wisdom,
Skill and tender care.
The blood that runs within your veins,
Is packed with color, too.
It is a part of God's nice way,
To say that He loves you.
So whether you are black or white,
Or brown or red or pink,
You are fortunately touched, friends,
With God's brilliant wonder ink.

And when the sun commences,
To sink in yonder western sky.
Rare beauty is displayed anew
To each beholding eye;
For sun and clouds, and sky and sea,
Are so lovely, as lovely as can be.
They seem transformed to works of art.
Thus they were meant to be.
From now, each time you chance
To see a lovely sunset,
Just stop a while and think,
That it is freely painted,
With God's brilliant wonder ink.

Repentance and Transformation

This Is What the Child of God Must Do
Luke 6:27–28

This is what the child of God must do.
This is what the child of God must do:
"Love your enemies." Love my enemies?
"Yes, this is what the child of God must do.
Bless those who curse you.
Do good to those who hate you.
Pray for those who spitefully use you
Pray for those who persecute You.

Rejoice; for this you must be glad.
Because of Me they make you sad.
For righteousness and My name's sake,
False accusations they do make.
Just know the kingdom will be thine.
Be merciful, be pure, be kind.
My servants who have gone before,
Suffered like things. You must endure.

This is what the child of God will do.
This is what the child of God will do.
If you'll be My sons indeed,
All My precepts you must heed.
When you're struck upon one cheek,
Turn the other and be meek."
This is what the child of God will do.
This is what the child of God will do.

Forget the pain that came your way.
Look forward to a brighter day.
Just keeping on walking with the Lord.
Keep on trusting in His word.
Then, help me thus, my light to shine,
In this darkened world of mine.
Then, to Thee shall be the praise.
And may men bless Your name always.

The Voice of Conscience
Acts 2:38

The voice of conscience is so loud,
To one single soul, or to a large crowd.

Some do not listen; pretend not to hear.
Others, they hearken, obeying with care.

Depression Breaker
Isaiah 51:11

Do you know where to go when depression sets in?
On your bended knees, the fight must begin.

Run to God to get some cover.
Don't let that monster take you over.

Bid Them Depart
Matthew 5:8

When thoughts pass quickly o'er my soul,
May I give God the full control
To do His work as does the sieve;
The bad to cast, the good to leave.

When evil thoughts come seeking
To dwell within your heart,
Through Christ they're not for keeping;
Just bid them all depart.

Plea for Comfort and Escape
Isaiah 43:2–3

The anguish of my heart is very great,
Encountering much strife and bitter hate.
I crave comfort, which only God can give,
As in this world I daily strive to live.

Lord, stand between me and my foes.
The sorrow they cause me overflows.
I pray, make a clear path for me,
Through this deep, distressing sea.

Men's Laws versus God's Compassion
1 Peter 2:13–14

If we transgress the law,
"Ignorance is no Excuse."
And we may have to pay a fine,
If some rule we abuse.

God's mercy is so different;
At our ignorance He winks.
He bestows on us compassion.
There's no greater love I think.

But while our God is winking,
He is waiting to see change;
So that our final destiny,
He'll gladly rearrange.

God's Transforming Power
1 Corinthians 6:11

Would God use a sinner like me,
So ashamed, and embarrassed, and unworthy?
When I think of my former life of sin,
Unless a new life with Christ I begin;

I will never be able to serve by His grace,
Unless I experience His forgiveness and peace.
But, when I think of Mary, and the dame at the well,
These reflections seem all my fears to dispel.

For it's marvelous what for them God had done.
How He saved and forgave them through His dear Son;
How He turned them around, and caused them to bless
A host of others, by what they confessed.

They realized Christ had saved them, and were not ashamed
To let others know what was wrought through His name.
And though I'm embarrassed, and sorely ashamed,
I thank God I am saved, through Christ's wonderful name.

Longing for Renewal
Isaiah 40:1

Though our beings be of dust,
Let our hearts learn to trust
In Thee, O God, forever.

And in that glorious day,
Change our earthly dust and clay,
To vessels that will
Praise Your Name for aye.

Repentance
Luke 13:2–3

A light turned on inside my head,
And there was a voice, which clearly said,
"You have wounded many hearts.
Might have torn their lives apart.

You've offended your Creator.
You have disobeyed your Maker."
That was quite a revelation,
That I failed at such temptations.

Lord, I willingly repent.
With this life I'm not content.
Now I need a brand-new head.
This old one's as good as dead.

And I need a brand-new heart.
I do need a better start.
And I need a brand-new life.
One that's free from all such strife.

And I want to please my Maker;
Obeying always, my Creator.
I don't want to make folks sad.
I would rather make them glad.

And I'm glad You passed my way.
Shed more light on me today.

Lord Put Enmity
Psalm 91:4

Lord, put enmity between sin and me.
Let me hate it, as it hates me.
Let me flee from it to Thee.

Let me be freed from its horrible grasp.
And let me be only Thine at last.

Train My Mind, O Lord
Ephesians 3:16–19

Train my mind, O Lord, today.
Mold it by Your will, I pray.
Heavenward let it bloom and grow,
Leaving dark and gloom below.

Bathe it in Thy holy light;
Let it think and act aright.
Let it love and kindness show;
Only purity to know.

Old bad habits chase away.
Let pleasantness and mercy stay.
Let it faith and hope employ.
Fill it with Your holy joy.

We Need True Repentance
Genesis 6:1–10

What do we need when we're naked,
When our spiritual bodies are bare?
When our actions are far from sacred,
When our sins to all others appear?

What do we need to bring us healing?
What do we need to hide our shame?
How can we hide what's revealing,
Causing disgrace to God's pure name?

We need to be honest with Jesus,
To truly repent of our sins;
For nothing we do can relieve us
From the shame or the shackles of sin.

We need the love of our Saviour.
We need His tender embrace;
For only His shed blood can cover
Our shame, or our sin's stains erase.

Our own solutions are futile.
Righteous pretensions won't do.
We need true conviction from heaven
The Spirit to search through and through.

Right about Face
Luke 12:15

There was a time I thought the lotto might be good,
And so I went and spent some bucks to win it if I could.
I figured if I won it, all the good things I could do.
It could solve a lot of problems, for myself and others, too.
But it only took away the money I had spent.
Then a nagging conscience somehow caused me to repent.

So I made a firm decision to be honest and content,
With the meager funds I now possess, and whatever God has sent.
And now I prefer to be poor, and to live by faith,
Which can lead me into heaven, where great treasures will be mine,
Forever and forever, not just for a little time;
Than to have a million dollars, and be left outside God's gate;

For God never said, He'll forsake us, just because we are poor.
And wealth is not a requisite, to enter heaven's door.
But giving God the honor, to sustain us day by day,
Is a better way to live on earth, until we pass away.
Then God will have the glory, and we will not be ashamed,
When Jesus comes to take us home, and this old earth reclaim.

Lord, help me while I live on earth, whether rich or poor,
To ever glorify Your name, and love You more and more.
And just like Paul and others, let me glory in Christ's cross,
And count all things but rubbish, and the wealth of earth as dross.

For I've gained a new perspective, of heaven's lasting wealth,
And the privilege of owning everlasting life and health,
That is filled with strength and vigor, and to be in company,
With all the saints and angels, and in fellowship with Thee,
And be blessed with Thee forever, throughout all eternity,
Where all Your saints are satisfied, and all are worry free.

Saul, Changed to Paul
Acts 9:1–31

Saul of Tarsus on the prowl;
Christians beaten and were hauled,
So the high priest could condemn,
Innocent and faithful men.

But it happened that one day,
Jesus met him on his way
To fetch souls who would be bound,
But he was arrested, and turned around,

By a bright light. Then he heard,
Words that were spoken by the Lord.
Christ said that Paul persecuted Him.
And there Paul's trouble did begin.

There he was told just what to do.
He had a job that was brand new.
He was called to preach to men,
Of Christ who died and lived again.

His career was now turned around.
He used to have the Christians bound.
His job was now to make men free.
He preached of Christ so fervently.

Jews and Gentiles were now told
That Jesus was the one foretold.
Who prophets spoke of years ago,
And now that truth they need to know.

What a great change wrought in Saul!
Hope that God would change us all.
From sinful and unworthy men.
To vessels fit to work for Him.

Reflections
Acts 1:8

There's a place behind the church's pulpit,
That I can see from the place where I sit.
What a delightful and wonderful place.
It seems to be bathed in glory and grace.

It glows with such a lovely hue,
As stained glass let the sunshine through.
I thought I was seeing a real flower bed,
With shrubs of green and flowers of red.

And upward projected a shining steel frame,
It seemed to glow and crowned with a flame.
I could not help but be thrilled with the view,
And wondered if others were seeing it, too.

But alas! As the sun went on its way,
The beautiful scenery faded away.
I wondered, where went that beautiful site.
And where is the flame and the flowers bright?

And then I thought of the Christian's life.
How it glows when reflecting God's light.
And how it can be all gloomy and gray,
When the Spirit of God is driven away.

The stained-glass window is like God's grace,
Which He can freely bestow on His saints.
And the Holy Ghost, like the glowing sun
Changes our lives, as He shines from within.

And saints like humble bushes, can flower
As on them God bestows His enabling power;
And like the structure which seems aflame,
They can glow when they trust in His name.

May I Likewise Live
John 6:7–8

Each Sabbath as I sit in church,
The Holy Spirit makes His search.
He turns on His reflecting beams,
And things just comes to light it seems.

And there I contemplate God's Word,
And meditate on what I've heard.
In church I'm His devoted child.
My manner and my words are mild.

Then I remembered; through the week,
I lost my patience, was not meek.
My temper overruled my mind,
And I said words that were not kind.

Now, Father, I forgiveness seek.
Please give me grace this coming week.
Just as You're in church with me today.
Henceforth, be with me every day.

Found at my duty, or my chore,
Or even at the grocery store,
May Thy sweet Spirit be felt there.
And make me then, Thy word to hear.

And every day in life's affairs,
When stresses steal in unawares,
Let me be calm and pleasant then,
So men can glorify Your name.

Help Me to Be Ready
Luke 12:40

Whenever I study God's Holy Word.
The "still small voice" of His Spirit is heard.
He helps me understand His promises true.
I know He will keep and fulfill them, too.

So this is now my great desire,
That to His kingdom I'll aspire.
This present world has nothing for me.
I long to be welcomed at the crystal sea.

Help me to be faithful in whatever I do.
Help me to be ready to go home with You.
Help me to stay in Your pathway narrow,
Even though in it, I experience sorrow.

Or although I'm beset by troubles wild,
Help me to be sober, calm, and mild.
And when there comes just woes on woes,
Help me remember You have taken my blows.

Help me to be ready when You come in power.
Help me to be ready for the judgment hour.
And whenever You come with Your angels all,
Help me to be ready for the trumpet call.

Sealed Forever
Revelation 7:1–3

The time may not be far from now,
When each will receive a seal on his brow,
So that some to God and to heaven will go,
And some will remain for the fire below.

When the righteous will righteous remain.
And the wicked will all stay the same.
Locked into whatever condition they're in;
Some righteous forever, some ruined by sin.

To decide for heaven, will then be too late.
However you are then, you'll stay in that state.
It's a truth indisputable, a truth so profound;
For heaven sealed, or for hell you'll be bound.

But what God desires is that all would repent,
And be saved through Christ, and our hearts rent.
That we would be part of His kingdom of peace,
To share His salvation, and join in His feast.

Christ's Return and Salvation

Praises to Our Coming King
Daniel 7:13–14

We are approaching judgment hour,
When Christ shall come with glory and power.
Quickly come and set us free.
How we long to be with Thee.

Let's prepare our hearts to meet Him.
All who turn from sin shall greet Him.
Let us thank Him for His grace.
We shall see Him face to face.

You are exalted on Your throne.
You shall reign, and You alone.
All other powers You shall put down.
You alone shall wear the crown.

All sleeping saints shall hear Your voice
All Your children shall rejoice.
All creation give You glory.
You alone are just and holy.

No More Sinkholes
Jeremiah 23:5–6

What's one of the latest, causing men to fear?
Seems as if the earth is opening up everywhere.
Seems as if we are not on solid ground;
Sinkholes now increasing, news of such abound.

There will be no sinkholes in Jerusalem.
Know for sure, the new earth will be rid of them
As we roam with Jesus, exploring all around,
Forever we'll be walking there, on solid ground.

Just as in the Bible it was then foretold;
All the streets beneath us will be solid gold.
With our blessed Jesus and the angels fair,
In God's holy presence, we shall have no fear.

And with the sure promise, Christ will come at last,
Sinkholes will surely be, something of the past.
And instead of us worrying, truly we'll rejoice;
Just because we listened, and obeyed His voice.

Let it now be told, to all the world around,
That all should be responding to the gospel's sound.
And instead of worrying, of sinkholes falling through.
Just shift your thoughts to Jesus coming back for you.

We Will Be Going to God's House
Mark 16:15

Hello, we'll be going to God's house one day.
And I want you to know, we'll be going to stay.
And that is why I knocked at your door,
To bring the good news you have not heard before.

We will be going—a numberless throng
Of folks who are saved; they'll be coming along.
And oh, how we all can hardly wait,
To see Abraham, father of those saved by faith.

Eager to see Jesus, the One first of all,
Who sent us, that we can give you a call.
He is so willing that you should be saved,
But you must be willing, and you must be brave.

You will gain entrance through Jesus the Lamb.
Don't keep Him waiting, come quickly along.
Come join the faithful and most joyful saints,
Whom our Father in heaven, gladly awaits.

People from all over the world will be there.
Who heard the good news, and dared to prepare.
We will be so happy, for we will be free
To live with our Saviour through eternity.

So will you accept the good news you have heard,
Surrendering to Jesus and His Holy Word;
Forsaking all things that would now come between,
And join with our Saviour and all the redeemed?

Heaven's Invitation
Revelation 22:17

Land and sea will give up the dead.
With the live saints they will all be led,
To heaven and the eternal shore,
To dwell with God forevermore.

They'll be gathered around God's throne,
Thanking Him for what He has done.
Oh, how I'm longing to be there,
Filled with joy, and peace, and cheer.

Aren't you longing to be there,
Where there's neither grief nor care?
God is bidding you to come,
To His everlasting home.

Oh, When?
Luke 12:37–38

Lord, when is Jesus coming back?
When will You send Him back to us?
He is the only One we trust.

Send Him quickly. Send Him soon
To His bride. She awaits her Groom.

Waiting Saints
Matthew 24:3–14

All Your saints are waiting, and praying,
And longing for Your return.
Of it they are speaking and singing,
Oh, how their hearts do burn.

They are hoping and yearning,
And they do discern,
That all the signs around them
Do speak of Your return.

I, too, await your coming.
I hope it will be soon.

Wise Choice Abraham Made
Hebrews 11:8–11

What a wise choice Abraham made
For living and survival.
The city which he longed for
Has no enemy or rival.

A place of peace where God is king,
Where joy will be forever.
And never will he roam again;
No earthly ties to sever.

I'm sure his heart will be so thrilled
To see his children there;
But most of all to see his Lord
Who'll welcome him with cheer.

Forgetting Earth and Its Ills
Isaiah 11:9

I'm glad that the ills of this earth,
Will not come to mind in heaven.
For that, I'm very glad today.
I'm glad it is arranged that way.

There will be so many things,
For us to do in heaven,
And many pleasures to Your saints,
In the new earth will be given.

Earth's devastating memories,
Will surely have no worth,
As saints enjoy the blessings,
That You'll give in the new earth.

Remembering earth's transient things,
Would surely spoil our joy.
So thank You, thank You very much,
That these will not annoy.

Transient versus Permanent Structures
Daniel 2:34–36

No structure on this earth is permanent,
Though to heaven their spires are sent.
Of low rise or high-rise which people may buy,
Skyscrapers or offices towering so high.

All are subject to erosion and subtle decay,
Tsunami or earthquake can floor them someday.
Termites or aging can all take their toll,
Or fierce storms, or fires, with actions more bold.

Let's not set our hearts on structures we own.
Sudden destruction can sure bring them down.
And, what earthly disaster does not take away,
Will all be consumed, in the great judgment day.

Let's keep our minds on God and on heaven,
And on permanent structures that we will be given.
Though their beauties are concealed from our eyes,
At the coming of Christ we'll be sweetly surprised.

Christ is preparing great mansions for us,
Made of the stuff that's not just earthly dust.
Their glory and beauty we'll gladly behold,
And inherit forever a city of gold.

Wake Up! The King Is Coming!
Romans 13:11–12

Wake up! The King is coming.
Soon will the trumpet sound.
He'll come in power and glory
To take His followers home.

Wake up! The King is coming.
So little time remains.
Recall the Savior's promise
That He will come again.

Wake up! The King is coming.
To gather up His own.
Awake from sleep and slumber.
Put on the wedding gown.

Wake up! The King is coming.
Soon comes the judgment day.
The books are now examined.
What do you have to say?

Wake up to spread the gospel
To all the waiting world.
Let sinners come to Jesus
While mercy still abounds.

Wake up! The King is coming.
The dead shall then arise.
Together with the waiting saints,
They'll meet Him in the skies.

We Shall Come with Gladness
Isaiah 35:10

We shall come with gladness;
We shall all rejoice.
When we see our Savior;
When we hear His voice.

All our woes shall vanish.
We're children of the King.
All heaven then rejoices
When of God's grace we sing.

Now as sons and daughters,
By heaven we are known.
We shall gladly gather
Around our Father's throne.

We our God adoring,
Dressed in robes of white;
Endless days enduring,
With our God of light.

Always a Servant
Matthew 24:45–46

In this life I'm just a servant.
I hold a common name,
No high status, and no fame.
I'm just a servant, just a servant.

And when Jesus comes again,
I'll be a servant just the same.
And while sailing through the air,
I guess I'll be a servant there.

And in the earth made new,
I will be a servant too.
Then, I'll be so very blessed.
I'll have joy and happiness.

And what honor that will be
If throughout eternity,
God wills this my post to be.
I'll be a servant, just a servant.

Christ Will Make Sure
Acts 4:12

Christ will make sure that we are there.
So do not worry. Have no fear.
He will make sure that we are saved,
Since His precious life He gave.

What a wonderful story!
We shall live with Him in glory.
Neither death, nor disease
Will prevent us, if you please.

There's no power, there's no might,
That can conquer in that fight,
But the Lord who reigns in glory.
What a wonderful story!

Let us now to Him draw near.
If we're faithful we'll be there.
All His promises He'll keep,
If we'll be His faithful sheep.

He will instantly dispel,
All the evil powers of hell.
Being saved from sin's tight grasp,
We shall live with Him at last.

He'll make sure we get to heaven,
Since His life for us He has given.
Never falter nor despair.
He'll make sure that we are there.

Accept God's Offers
Romans 1:18–21

This world is so unstable,
With earthquakes, storms, and wars;
And illnesses, men disabled,
And crimes our cities mar.

Floods bury our possessions,
And carry our wealth away.
We lose our crops and livestock,
And families in one day.

We mourn our sudden losses,
Which bring to us dismay;
And as we rise to build again,
Winds blow it all away.

Oh, we should reconsider,
The invitation God has given,
To make Christ the Lord our shelter,
And secure a home in heaven.

There we'll know of no disasters,
No homeless on the streets.
No wars, or crimes, or illnesses,
There, experiences are sweet.

So hear God's invitation,
And rest content today.
Accept the homes in heaven,
He freely gives away.

Accept God's Offers (continued)

With homesteads so enduring,
And not a dime to pay,
How could you turn God's offer down,
And coldly walk away?

Look beyond earth's oft disasters,
Embrace God's care and love,
For earth's woes and troubles
Will give way to blessings above.

Heavenly Train
Colossians 1:13–14

Heavenly train, heavenly train,
From that place whence Jesus came;
Come and take us to the same,
Take us there in Jesus' name.

Heavenly train, heavenly train,
Oh, return to earth again.
Come and bear God's saints to glory,
To that place so pure and holy.

Heavenly train, heavenly train,
Bring God's Son to earth again.
Bring the Son of God most lowly;
Let Him come in all His glory.

Earthly Problems Light and Gone
2 Corinthians 4:6–8

We think our earthly problems
Are enormous with great weight.
We feel that they will weigh us down,
And thus may seal our fate.

But take heart, my dear ones,
Don't let them weigh you down,
Just know that help is coming,
And that we are heaven bound.

And know the time is coming,
When we will be trouble free,
When these earthly troubles,
Will seem light as light can be.

Just know your pesky problems,
That you now have to endure,
Will then seem as light as feathers
When you reach the other shore.

This Earth Neither Safe nor Permanent
Revelation 21:1

Father, You know that this old earth
Is not the place to be.
We're plagued by fierce tornadoes,
And storms on land and sea.

We scarcely get a break from these
Before we hear of wars.
Death and destruction seem the norm.
We're plagued by dreadful disease.

It is time that we come to know,
That this old earth is vain.
It's neither safe nor permanent,
Until Christ comes again.

Prepare for us again an ark.
That we can head for heaven.
Our Savior, Jesus Christ the Lord,
The Ark, that You have given.

God Shall Make Our Bodies Anew
1 Corinthians 15:50–52

The devil smote Job with a grievous sore,
Thinking Job would not serve God anymore.
But Job kept on trusting God anyway.
He was sure that he would see God someday.

He knew that worms his skin could destroy.
But yet he knew he could see God with joy.
He insisted that he would patiently wait,
To answer to God's call, in a renewed state.

And so his integrity, he calmly maintained,
Though he suffered through distress and pain.
By his faith he proved the devil untrue.
And we know God will make Job's body anew.

When David was struck with offensive sores.
His acquaintances came not nigh anymore
Because he had this loathsome disease,
Which all the while gave him no ease.

But David never lost faith in God.
He still extolled and cherished the Lord.
He kept on praising God anyway,
And in his affliction, continued to pray.

David shall someday reap his reward,
For having such firm faith in his God.
And like Job, he shall live again,
All freed from sorrow, and sores, and pain.

I also shall see my Redeemer someday.
When all my diseases shall be taken away.
No foul odor here, no foul odor there.
No diseased condition to pollute the air.

God Shall Make Our Bodies Anew (continued)

I will be smelling as sweet as a rose.
No offensive odor to annoy any nose.
At the resurrection, to me God shall give
Everlasting life. By His grace shall I live.

Yes, it is true. This will God do.
He shall make my body anew.
Let's sing, rejoice, and praise God anyway,
Until our breath shall be taken away.

Now, if you have some loathsome disease,
And day nor night you have no ease.
If you have Jesus; even though you may die,
He'll raise you in a moment, take you on high.

You'll never experience suffering again.
There will be no sickness, suffering or pain.
Yes, it is true. This will God do.
He shall make our bodies anew.

They Shall Behold His Glory
John 17:11–13, 24

When Jesus came to earth,
He singled out twelve men,
To help Him with the kingdom
He wanted to build then.

They gladly hearkened to His call;
Went everywhere with Him.
They gladly made the sacrifice,
And did the work begin.

And as He gently nurtured them,
In love and faith they grew.
And there came a time fortunately, when,
They became His helpers and loyal friends.

Sadly, one of them betrayed his Lord,
But all the others stood firm and were true.
When Christ was attacked they were forlorn.
But recovered and began their work anew.

And since Jesus knew they would loyal be,
His glory in heaven He wanted them to see.
So upon His Father He began to call,
To bestow this blessing upon them all.

And how happy those disciples will be,
When in time Christ's glory they shall see.
I believe they'll again their Lord adore,
And will gratefully praise Him evermore.

God's Strength and Guidance

Walking with Jesus
Matthew 28:20

Our walk with Jesus can be pleasant and sweet,
As we heed His precepts and sit at His feet.
It is a pleasure to hear His sweet voice,
Which makes our hearts and beings rejoice.

And He will be with us wherever we roam;
Through trials, or troubles, or whatever may come.
We'll all be contented, and satisfied too,
For He will be guiding in all that we do.

Early Let Me Rise
Psalm 5:1-3

Early, Father, let me rise,
Turn my eyes unto the skies.

Take all hindrances away.
Let me serve You through this day.

Who Am I Really Serving on the Job?
Colossians 3:22–24

Is it just my boss I serve
While working on the job?

No. In addition to my wages,
God gives me a reward.

God Has Something to Say Every Day
Psalm 40:6

If you listen every day,
You'll hear God has more things to say.
He will not mislead you.
He will never guide you wrong.

If you listen to his voice
He'll drive your gloom away.
And if His will becomes your choice,
You will be strong for aye.

Lift Me and Guide Me
Proverbs 3:5–8

Lord lift me out of the dumps today,
For I am feeling low.
Let me be prepared to help,
Wherever I may go.

You're my true companion.
Whisper words of love.
Lift me up from my distress,
And let me look above.

I know that You are truly,
The healer of my soul.
Ever be the great guide of
My hopes, and plans, and goals.

Oh, How Can We Serve?
Hebrews 12:1

Oh, how can we serve our God now?
Will someone please tell us how?
Young folks can choose to steal away,
Get on their knees, wrestle, and pray.

If you are old, it's still all right;
Surely, old warriors can still fight,
As long as God gives strength and might.
We all need to be strong and bold,
Just like the righteous men of old.

Some were weak, then became strong,
Through trust, and struggling hard and long.
Some were cast down, but got up again.
'Twas God who helped them through their pain.

Could have given up; but they did not.
They kept on fighting;
'Twas their lot.
So how can we serve our God now?
Are we still asking, "Oh, just how?"

On bended knees we'll cry, and cry,
'Till God sends strength from heaven on high.

Jesus, Our Dear Savior
John 3:17

We learn of our dear Savior,
Who lived so long ago.
He came to earth to save us,
Whom now by faith we know.

We heard that children praised Him.
Disciples heard His call.
And now we want to serve Him,
The "One who died for all."

We want to be more like You
In everything we do.
So give us grace, and power,
And strength, to always honor You.

Out of a Hard Day
Hebrews 10:32–36

Out of a hard day comes a song.
After fierce battles, victories won.

In spite of our weaknesses,
We are made strong.

Out of our distresses,
Faith has suddenly sprung.

God Woos Us in the Morning
Psalm 5:3

God woos us in the morning,
As soon as we awake;
Inviting us to come to Him,
And of His blessings take.

And yes, there comes conviction,
For all the wrongs we've done;
But still He gently woos us,
And forgives us through His Son.

And as we leave His presence,
Filled with peace and joy,
Our burdens seem to vanish,
And nevermore annoy.

Recognizing and Trusting Christ
James 1:12

Chosen by God, they trusted in Christ's name.
They recognized Him, when to earth He came.
And others through the ages, trusted in His Word,
'Though they were tormented or killed with the sword.

May we in this present age, bravely follow on,
And cling to our Savior, though persecutions come.
To all such believers, God has promised a reward.
So let us then resolve to be faithful to the Lord.

Do We Really Know?
Romans 8:16–17

Do we really know,
Or do we really care,
That God is our Father;
That we are counted heirs?

Do we want the blessings,
That our God bestows;
Or do we want to gather,
With His wily foes?

We should all be thinking,
Of our Father's love.
We should all be longing,
For the joys of heaven above.

Come, sweet Holy Spirit,
Tell us so we yearn,
For that love that's for us,
Let's accept it in return.

We are void of knowledge.
Yes, we do not know.
Assist us to receive that love,
That God on us bestows.

Let All Heaven Now Rejoice
Psalm 40:1–3

I will accept and follow Christ.
To live for Him, this is my choice,
So let all heaven now rejoice.

I love the Lord with all my heart.
Troubles cannot rend us apart.
After all the social shock,

After all the enemy's mock;
I say "God is on His throne;
And I know that I'm His own."

After my poor heart was torn,
After I've been trapped and caught,
By the wiles the oppressor wrought;

I say "God is on His throne;
And I know that I'm His own."

God's salvation is my all.
He lifted me when I did fall.
Cleansed me in the precious blood,
Of Jesus Christ my Saviour and Lord.

I have made the final choice,
So let all heaven now rejoice.

I love the Lord with all my heart.
Lord keep me close and let's not part.

No evil power can keep me bound.
I'll wear the overcomer's crown,
And a new white wedding gown.

A new name God will give to me,
And I'll praise Him through eternity.

Trust God Always
Psalm 10:16–18

Though you go through fire and flood,
If you have faith, rejoice in God.
Still trust Jesus. Never doubt,
Eternity's what life's about.

Trust in Jesus, never cease.
He will give you "lasting peace."
That is, if you'll trust in Him,
If you'll make Him Lord and King.

Prayer for Rest
Ecclesiastes 5:12

Please Jesus; all our burdens keep.
Take all our cares, so we can sleep.

We need to be refreshed and strong;
To rise and praise You with a song.

So let us sleep the whole night through.
On waking we'll give thanks to You.

May We Escape Sin's Entrapment
Proverbs 4:14–17

The wicked do not sleep at all,
Unless they cause some soul to fall.
The righteous seek to do men good,
For God requires that they should.

The wicked are bound for hell's fire.
The righteous will to heaven aspire.
Wicked men shall pass away
The righteous will endure for aye.

God can deliver from sin's traps.
It is not maybe, or perhaps.
Oh may we see, and thus discern,
Entrapment, and from it to turn,

Before, we stumble and thus fall.
So may we learn on God to call;
For falling can produce much stain,
That on our consciences remain.

Lord, let our consciences be free.
And may our lives be pure for Thee.
Instead of being entrapped by sin,
May we be vessels, pure and clean.

My Best Friend
Psalm 136:26

Jesus my Lord is such a friend;
His love is constant; knows no end.
He saw me lying by the road,
Broken and battered, bruised and torn.

He cared for me with loving hands.
Poured oil and wine into my wounds.
Gently He carried me to rest,
Where pain and harm would not molest.

I did not hear condemning words.
Only His love and pity flowed
To calm my griefs and fears within.
That's why I trust my heart to Him.

Friendship and Family Matters

To My Sister Ethel
Proverbs 16:24

You made my first birthday cake;
You did it just for pure love's sake.
Years have passed, you give me still,
Sometimes, a hundred-dollar bill.

Remembering your love and sacrifice,
Brings me much joy, and I rejoice.
I thank you for the precious birthday gift,
But most of all, your words gave me a lift;

For I felt down, before your letter came.
I know you did it all in Jesus' name.
Yes, we are drawing near to "sunset" time.
All we need now is love, both yours and mine.

Yes, I was deeply touched by your kind words.
I know that God is pleased by what He heard.
Keep on giving, oh my sister true.
The love you give will come right back to you.

Prayer for Air Travel Safety
Psalm 50:15

God, be with crew and pilot.
Please guide us through the air;
All through storm or sunshine,
Let us feel You near.

Quell all interruptions,
And dispel our fears.
Be with other travelers,
In the vast airways.

Bring us to our homes again,
Whether through dark clouds or rain.
When brought back to carefree days,
May Your holy name be praised.

When Facing Threat or Harm
Isaiah 41:10

Heavenly Father, please protect us,
From those who would do us harm.
Grant us Your peace, and help us to be calm.
Help us to trust You and be not afraid.
By Your mighty arm and power,
In the time of harm and threat,
Lend us then, Thine aid.

Prayer for Safety Away from Home
Psalm 17:6–7

As we leave our homes today,
Keep us safe, we humbly pray.
And when we head back home,
Be with us all the way.

Hide us in the shadow
Of Your mighty wings.
Fold us in your warm embrace;
You're our mighty King.

You're our loving Father,
And may we always be,
Your faithful trusting children,
Only Yours forever, to eternity.

Teach Us How to Love
Ephesians 4:32

Father, teach us how to love
Mortals on earth and Thee above.
To love those who cause us sore distress,
And those who bring us happiness.

To love the pleasant, and the mean;
The lowly peasant, king, or queen.
We find it hard to truly love,
Mortals on earth, as Thee above.

We know not how to love at all.
We know though, how to build a wall
To keep all pain and sorrow out,
Which cause us oft to fret and doubt.

So change us now, that we may know,
Just how to love our foes below.
That You may give us perfect love,
To love mankind and Thee above.

Morning Exercise Booster

3 John 2

We swing our arms, we take deep breaths.
We are such happy creatures. Yes!
Sun on face, the day begun.
We hop and skip, and jump and run.

Sun illuminates the face.
Now we want to run a race.
We exercise where'er we go,
That hearts can pump and blood can flow.

Exercise where ever we are at,
So we'll be thin, and not be fat.
We do not want to be too thin,
For there our troubles will begin.

Healthy muscles and strong bones
Is our real goal. May this be done.
And our minds should fervent be,
Engaging friends or family.

Waiting for You
Galatians 6:2

I hoped your nimble, little feet,
The pathway to my house would beat.

Longingly I waited for you,
To help me shed a tear or two;

But you're not coming round the bend.
You're not showing, oh, my friend.

Now you're coming round the bend.
Now you're coming, oh, my friend,

To help me shed a tear or two.
Now you are proved a friend so true.

Reciprocated Love
John 15:12

God loves me, and I love thee.
And what can make our spirits free,

Is if you would my love discern,
And come to love me in return.

God's Commands versus Satan's Lies
1 Peter 5:8

As Eve and Adam disobeyed,
We do the same today;
Ignoring plans which God outlined,
Not following what He says.

God made a woman and a man;
To multiply. That was His plan.
Offspring from both should fill the earth.
This only could occur through birth.

And now we see the evil one,
Tempting man to change God's plan.
Male and male are marrying now.
Women with women exchanging vow.

Now, man with man, cannot produce.
Woman with woman, can't bear fruit.
This plan comes from the evil one,
To undermine Jehovah's plan.

And if this practice we pursue,
The earth will soon be bare.
You would not want that to occur,
Unless you do not care.

So let us God's pure plan embrace.
Let us preserve the human race,
By marrying male to a female.
This is God's plan. Let it not fail.

Some think that it's just people,
Who are telling them what to do.
But that is truly God's idea,
Laid down for me and you.

God's Commands versus Satan's Lies (continued)

Surely, we should take the blame,
For drifting far from Him;
For choosing what results in shame,
And courting death through sin.

But it's not right to kill the ones,
Deceived by Satan's lies.
Like you, they need time to repent,
And change before they die.

God truly loves everyone He makes.
And for us, His heart does truly ache.
He also wants His subjects to repent.
That is why to us, His Spirit He has sent.

And we should know, that only God is judge.
He also has the perfect plan, to save us by His love.
That is why He sent His Son, to redeem our souls,
For that's the only way, that He could make us whole.

In dust and ashes, let's repent.
To live in sin, be not content.
We will be guiltless if we do.
And we should stand for what is true.

Lord, by your Spirit let us know,
The traps laid down by our great foe
That we should not your law fulfill,
Walking contrary to Your will.

May we all live by Your designs,
Instead of following sin's ensigns.
Our spiritual eyes at times are blurred.
And our decisions so absurd.

Please send Your Spirit upon us.
Open our eyes to righteousness.

God's Commands versus Satan's Lies (continued)

All Your commandments are so pure.
Your testimonies are so sure.

Teach us to listen to Your voice.
Let your will be our only choice.
Forgive our errors of the past,
And save us by Your grace at last.

Take all the blindness from our eyes.
Take pity; for to You we cry.
We really want to do Your will.
Within our hearts Your law instill.

For all our frailties give us strength.
And let us now truly repent,
Avoiding Sodom's awful fate.
Escaping ere it be too late.

Please let Your Spirit lead and guide,
Until we're gathered by Your side;
Where disobedience will not be,
Forever, through eternity.

Why Did God Make Woman and Man?
Genesis 1:27–28

God made a woman and a man,
To reproduce and fill the land;
Numberless becoming, as the sand.

To man, that first command was given
By Him who made the earth and heaven.
As time went on, seemed men forgot,
And so their numbers shrank a lot.

They took matters into their own hands,
And so devised "The Family Plan."
They said, "Many children we can't feed,
Since that will bring distress and need."

But God can bless a small amount;
Though, man would rather fear and doubt.
God's word can produce lots of food,
To feed a hungry multitude.

Let's not be scared God's word to try,
And see what He does by and by;
For when He speaks, His Word is done.
That's how His universe is run.

If only we His Word would heed,
We'd have no fear, and know no need.

Infants' Pleas and Moms' Resolve
Luke 1:11–16

If infants could only speak,
Just what would they say?
"Our lungs are tender,
And we're weak.

Please don't smoke, we pray."
And moms while carrying
Them would say,

"We'll not live carelessly,
We'll be drug free.
We'll be smoke free.
For our precious babies.

We've seen the harm
That smoke and drugs
Have done, to our dear children
So we'll refrain from using these.

May God's blessing be upon them."
To be drug free, to be smoke free
Should be all moms' resolve,
And not to live so carelessly,
But giving care, and much love.

Wives, Wives, Be Alive!
Proverbs 31:10–31

Wives, wives, be alive.
Sing God's praises if you're wise.
Read the scriptures. Meditate.
Everyone should live by faith.

Say your prayers. Get out of bed.
Start to work. You are not dead.
There are burdens you must bear,
After you have said your prayers.

Clean the house. Feed your spouse.
To your job, and work some more.
If you don't, you will be poor.
Be more mild. Train your child.

Wash the clothes. Plant a rose.
Love your kin. Never sin.
Listen, eh? Just obey.
Early rise. Exercise.

Serve all others. Make them smile;
Then sit down and rest a while.
Where are you going? Not so fast.
You must know that you're the last.

Mow the lawn and trim the trees.
Grow some flowers for the bees.
Feed the dog, and stroke the cat.
You must never get too fat.

Do something for charity.
Be as kind as you can be.
Do some handshakes. Call a friend.
I wonder when this thing will end?

Get some groceries while you shop.
Make your children smile a lot.
I see you're always on the run.
Now you can stop. Your work is done.

Money Flies
Proverbs 10:4

My money seems to fly away
Though I never saw its wings.
And seems to stay but for a day,
Like some unstable things.

Not much of it I ever saved.
It always flies away.
I guess it's made for spending,
And for bills and debts to pay.

And on your tireless journey,
Bless some widow on the way,
And hungry children who now cry
For food throughout the day.

The Ruins of Gossip
Leviticus 19:16

Gossip maims. Yes, gossip kills.
Gossip causes lots of ills;
Ruins friendships, tears up homes,
Leaves some feeling all alone.

Oh how gossip makes one blue,
When it tells tales that are not true.
It breeds distrust and malcontent,
And hammers until hearts are rent.

Can devastate a family,
And, oh, how cruel it can be.
It causes ruin in its path,
And sets in motion hate and wrath.

Envy is its constant friend.
What it destroys is hard to mend.
It's subtle, and it causes pain.
It does result in loss, not gain.

And when it's done it leaves a wreck,
For what it starts is hard to check.
And thus it rages on and on,
Until its victims are all gone.

One wonders when such rage would end,
And prays to God His grace to send;
So those who gossip would now find
The grace to let their words be kind.

Tolerate the Children
Mark 10:13–16

Let's give children a helping hand,
And help their parents all we can.
Let us help to soothe their fears,
Instead of causing needless tears.

Jesus is asking this of us.
It is required. It's a must.
Let's be patient as we go along.
To Christ it will be a happy song.

Although they need good discipline,
Let us find pleasant ways our children to win.
True, if we correct them, they will not die.
They will bring us honor, not shame, by and by.

And although we should be outspoken and firm,
Remember Christ said, to Him they should come.
We need more patience. We need more to pray.
That God will guide as we show them the way.

Never Woman Without Man
Genesis 1:27

There was never woman without man,
For she was taken out of man.

Bone of man's bone, flesh of man's flesh;
By God's decree, forever after to mingle and mesh.

Jesus Also Cares
James 5:19–20

I made my way through doors and locks,
To get to our letter box.
And then at last I did not fail,
To find even one piece of mail.

One piece of mail? Now let me see.
This piece of mail belongs to me.
It is a yellow envelope.
Good news therein? Well, that I hope.

I broke that yellow envelope to see,
 Just what good news it held for me.
A card! Of this I was surprised.
And such good news it had inside!

And as I read its short contents,
My heart was glad. I was content.
It said someone was glad to see me
Back in church where I should be.

And does not Jesus also care,
When from the fold we stray?
With open arms, He welcomes us,
Back to the narrow way.

May It Go Well
Psalm 91

Lord, may it go well
On the playground today.
Bless all these dear children,
As they frolic and play.

Let them keep from the thickets,
For they might be pricked
By thorns that are sharp,
Or may fall on sharp sticks.

May they stay in the open,
Where they will be in sight.
May they stay in the warm sun,
And share its bright light.

May their muscles develop,
May they grow big and strong.
As they swing bats, or throw balls,
Or go skipping along.

Help them to be careful,
As they climb bars so high,
When they get on the swings,
Or jump toward the sky.

Help them to be refreshed,
As they breathe in the air.
Give them more vigor,
As they run everywhere.

May the big boys and girls,
Be as kind as can be,
To each frail little child,
They may happen to see.

(continued)

May It Go Well (continued)

Please keep them from falling,
Please shield them from harm.
And in case of some mishap,
Let the teachers be calm.

As the storms start to gather,
Let them run from the trees
To the safety of the schoolhouse,
Or some hiding place, please.

Take them to their classes,
Safe and sound, and intact,
To listen to their teachers,
As they teach them new facts.

Children Like to Play
Matthew 18:2–3

Although children like to play,
There should be time during the day
When they are given things to do,
That will teach skills and wisdom, too.

After they laugh and skip and hop
And have their fun with jumping rope,
After the see-saw and the swing
Then some learning should begin.

They can have fun reading books
And eat the food that Mother cooks.
They should also learn to pray,
For that will come in good someday.

If they are in danger or alone,
They can pray that help will come.
Teach them to use the telephone,
And when in danger, to call home.

For as we live more and more,
Playing now is not like before.
For as we played and ran around,
Everyone was safe and sound.

We hardly had to lock our doors,
Now children aren't safe anymore.
For we turn aside, and they are gone.
And then the parents' hearts are torn.

But children still need to play,
To frolic, laugh, and scream away,
To strengthen muscles, lungs, and bones.
For their good health, in days to come.

Mothers, Be Alert!
Matthew 18:10–11

Mothers be alert. Mothers be alert.
How much are your lost items worth?
Please linger near. Do not go very far.
We have items for a Lost and Found Bazaar.

It could be that we have items that you seek.
We have things that were left here for weeks.
We have racquets, balls, gloves, mittens, hats,
Sweaters and scarves, in our lost and found box.

We've collected the things which were lying around,
So we hope that your precious things can be found.
Just come and see. You can have them at no cost.
Hope you will recover the things that were lost.

So be here tomorrow promptly at four.
Someone will be here to greet you at the door.
Follow the blue line. It will show you where we are.
Hope you will be happy at our Lost and Found Bazaar.

Your precious children are souls that can be lost,
But Jesus came to save them forever, at no cost.
So Mothers, you must cooperate with God's plan,
In prayer on your knees, and Bibles in your hands.

And if you will take heed to the Savior's voice,
Someday soon, you and your children will rejoice.
For Jesus is coming back, and that day is not far,
When we'll celebrate the best Lost and Found Bazaar.

God's Uniqueness

Love Song
John 15:12

Love is what our Lord commands.
United in love, your souls will bond;
And by this the world will know,
You're My disciples when love you show.
Love You desire that we should gain;
But how shall we this love obtain?
Now we beseech Thee, Lord above,
Send us this sweet, unblemished love.

"'Twas by that sweet love I came;
Served by love in My Father's name.
By that love I served and died,
Yes, by that love I was crucified.
And by that love I will come again.
By that love I'll forever reign.
And throughout eternity,
My love will abide, oh saints, for thee."

Oh, 'twas by love that Jesus came,
Served by love in His Father's name.
By love He served, with love he died.
Yes, for our love He was crucified.
And with love He comes again.
By this love He'll forever reign.
And throughout all eternity,
His love will abide for you and me.

Love of the Father, love of the Son,
Love of the Spirit, Three in One!
How They do unite to bestow,
Love to their children here below.
Now love for our brethren, Father, send;
Love for all 'til time shall end;
Love, O Lord our God, to thee,
Now and throughout eternity.

God Makes Wonderful Things
Psalm 40:5

Oh, what wonderful things God has made.
And He made them all without our aid.
He made the great big swimming whale,
And the lowly complex kale.

We know of the complexity
Of our live human body.
And water seems so very plain,
But on examining it again,

It's made of more than we can see.
And so is every living tree,
And the tiny honeybee,
And flowers; they're a sight to see.

Examine fruits before you eat.
They are complex, and most are sweet.
Bananas and strawberries are marvels, too,
If they are examined by slicing them through.

Many fruits are just readymade pies.
God made them for us. What a surprise!
But we just eat them and go on our way,
Not acknowledging miracles, sent day by day.

Let's thank God for pies placed on the tree,
And all the wonders made for you and me.
But talking of it from dawn until sunset,
We would not have touched the half of it yet.

God's Love Seen in What He Has Made
Genesis 1:1

Look around and see the verdant trees,
With their branches and their lively leaves.
See them waving in the passing breeze.
All God's works are surely made to please.

See the white clouds against the azure sky,
Awesome scenes as they go passing by.
God has made them. That we can't deny.
We breathe a prayer of thankfulness as they pass by.

And if you chance to see the ocean's waves,
They proclaim the love of God who saves.
For He has set a bound that keeps them in,
As by His law and word, protecting us from sin.

Everything of land, and sea, and air,
Are made by Him and show His tender care.
And since we've come to know who placed us here,
Let's praise Him willingly with love and godly fear.

God Is, and Will Always Be Alive
Revelation 1:18

Some say God is dead, but in all the world around,
Evidences He exists, are not hard to be found.
Such a theory my friends, does not make any sense.
It is time for you to stop, and explore the evidence.

And though we cannot see Him,
Does not mean He is not there.
And He is always willing
Our concerns and prayers to hear.

God is not dead my doubting friends.
He will always be alive.
He's longing that one day, you'll come
To join Him in the skies.

Miracle Divine
1 John 1:7

Red blood making my sins white as snow.
How this is done, I do not know.

It is a miracle all divine,
That Christ's blood has cleansed
This sinful heart of mine.

God Alone Is Love
Jeremiah 31:3

Only our great God above,
Can claim the precious name of Love.
Earthly monarchs, queens, and kings,
Who own a zillion precious things,
And are adored by free and slave,
Oft fleeting love to humans gave.

God's love is pure, and thus it lasts
For generations to all class.
Who else compared to all of these
Have made the earth, the skies, the seas?
And constantly God does men good;
Distributes water, air, and food.

We see in this that "God is Love."
None else in earth or heaven above
Could claim that precious name of love.
Though conquerors are great and strong,
To God alone that name belongs.

Who else of guardians, kings, or queens
Give love to all created beings?
Let's revel in the love of God,
And praise Him now with one accord.

Let's thank Him for the Virgin Birth,
The One who came to show God's love
To all His subjects here on earth.
Yes, only our great God above,
Can claim the precious name of Love.

God Hears and Understands Our Prayers
Romans 8:26–27

God heard the prayers of men of yore;
Of saints who prayed from hearts so pure.
He hears the prayers of strong and weak,
Prayers uttered oft by those who're meek.

Sometimes we feel too weak to pray,
And often know not what to say.
But with utterance to men unknown,
The Spirit bears them to God's throne.

It matters not your words are few,
If they spring forth from motives true.
God listens still with great delight,
As heavenward they wing their flight.

And I'm so glad God understands
Our stumbling words not clear to man.
May we take comfort as we pray,
Though God may seem so far away;

And know that Christ does intercede,
As we to God doth daily plead,
And make petitions, great or small,
Since we know that He hears them all.

God Is a Good God
Exodus 34:5–7

God is a good God, a kind God, a loving God,
A gracious God, a forgiving God.
God is a good God, a kind God, a loving God,
A gracious God, a forgiving God.

I know it, for I was lost in sin,
Uncomely without, and impure within.
He gave me what I did not deserve.
Forgiveness for sins, when death I deserved.

Though my friends loved me with reserve,
It was not so with the God I serve.
In times of my failures He came to me.
He gave me comfort so tenderly.

He said, "I've forgiven all your sins,
You'll be radiant without, and be pure within.
You know I'm a God who freely forgives.
Overcome and be faithful, and with Me you shall live."

Although from me, people turn away,
My God stays with me both night and day.
And no, He will never leave me alone.
He will stay with me till his Kingdom comes.

God is a good God, a kind God, a loving God,
A gracious God, a forgiving God.
God is a good God, a kind God, a loving God,
A gracious God, a forgiving God.

God Loves the Handicapped
Isaiah 32:3–4

God loves the handicapped. He does.
And Jesus showed to them God's love,
When He says to them, "Rise up and walk,"
Or when He with compassion,
Caused the mute to talk.

And when He comes again to reign,
He'll bid them rise and live again.
Yes, when they hear His blessed voice,
All the broken will rejoice.

God Has Made All Things for Good
Genesis 1:29

God has made all things
For good and not for evil,
But man has taken some of them
And used them for the devil.

Take for instance, technology;
What a blessing that can be.
When it's used in such a way
To save or set men free.

It is time for us just to review,
How God's gifts we use.
If with them we do bless the world,
Or subjecting them to abuse.

May God bless those who enhance life,
And not cause pain and fret.
Since God made all things for our good.
And not for our death.

God's Touch
Matthew 8:1–3

God's touch is so sublime;
It makes man's face to shine.
And though His touch can make the waters part,
His tender touch can mend the broken heart.

God's touch can make the blind to see.
His touch can cause the dumb to speak.
That touch which made the lepers clean,
Is the same touch that cleanses us from sin.

Spiritual Food Is the Best
Psalm 119:125

Lord, You filled the earth with physical food,
But You also gave us Your Word, which is good.
We tend to hunger for physical bread,
Then quickly forget what to us You have said.

Let us hunger, then feed on Your words so divine.
To sit at Your feet, let us all be inclined.
Some eat physical food and are filled with pride
Then go on to declare that Your "law is void."

Let us not wholly on physical food depend,
Seeing that the physical will come to an end.
It is only by Your Word that we will be set free;
And Your law will last through eternity.

God Made Various Things from the Same Soil
Genesis 1:26

God formed man of the dust of the earth,
And made him into a being of worth.
In this God's wisdom and power is seen;
Man from soil, then man to being.

From this old earth that we've come to know,
God causes different things to grow.
The earth sends forth trees strong and tall,
And from it, bushes low and small.

Hardwood trees, and shrubs, and vines;
Grass and moss, and trees with spines.
Some furnish us with homes secure,
While some we use, our ills to cure.

God clad most with colors of green,
And other colors our eyes have seen.
And various fruits, some trees would bear.
What other power could place them there?

Diverse fruits, and diverse flowers,
Animals and man, with all their colors.
It is wonderful what God can do.
His wisdom perfectly shines through.

Bringing them all from the same soil,
As they emerge, all without toil.
Then God gave His creations to man.
Thank God! Let's enjoy them all we can.

Jesus' Name Lives On
Revelation 5:13–14

Jesus' name lives on, and on, and on.
It was there from the beginning; God's beloved Son.
It was there from ages past,
And will linger till the last,
When time its course has run.

Yes, God's everlasting Son's name,
Will be sounding just the same.
What a name! Creating, life-giving,
Powerful, gracious, precious,
Living on, and on, and on.

God Does Great Things
Titus 2:11–14

God always does great things,
And He has more great things to do.
Do not be surprised my friends,
If His next act is "changing you."

I'll welcome His performance
Of reconstructing me;
To fill my heart with peace and grace,
And feet from sin to flee,

Construct my mind, and my desires
To yearn for things above,
And grant me wisdom to inspire
The world with truth and love.

Nebuchadnezzar's Dream
Daniel 2:1–45

Nebuchadnezzar, filled with awe;
First he thought, and then he saw.
'Twas God who gave to him that dream,
But he forgot what he had seen.

God sent Daniel to explain the plan,
Which heaven had for mortal man.
It was not just for the king alone,
For God had plans for other thrones.

God showed him what the plans would be,
From his time to eternity;
Of kingdoms which would rise, then fall.
And he was the first of them all.

There was a kingdom yet to come,
Which all the saints would call their home.
Where God Himself their king would be,
Forever through eternity.

Sometimes we have to let dreams go.
But in time, God lets us know,
On what dreams He has placed His seal,
As He, His plans to men reveals.

God's Sunshine and Rain
Psalm 19:4–6

Sometimes we despise rainy days,
And hope the sun would shine always.
We do not like when it is wet.

It causes us to fuss and fret.
And if the sun gets very hot,
We also will complain a lot.

We need the sunshine and the rain.
From both many blessings we can gain.

We just need wisdom to prepare,
For the cloud's rain, or the sun's flare.

Comes pouring rain, or glaring sun,
It is God's blessing that is done.

And the simple fact remains,
That we are both by these sustained.

God's Life-Sustaining Air
Genesis 2:7

Whence came the wind, and whither does it go?
It remains invisible, for God has made it so.
Of all the earth's elements, the wind we cannot tame.
It goes to and fro, but it still remains the same.

If only men could catch and tame the precious air.
It would be only used in ways that is not fair.
For if we caught the wind, we would never let it go.
It would no more be free to travel to and fro.

And it would be kept to be exchanged for gold.
But life was not intended to be bought or to be sold.
God has reserved the air, for His creatures all to live.
And life as we know it, is only His to give.

So thank You, Father, for Your wisdom that is fair;
That all accesses freely that valuable air.
For if some could control it, only they would live.
But from our Life-giver, this gift we've all received.
And now I am so thankful for such a loving God,
Who bestowed upon us all, His gifts of life and love.

Why I Believe in God
Psalm 96:1–6

I believe in You, O God. Lord,
I believe in You.
If I must talk, or eat, or breathe,
Living breath from You I need.

When this world first began,
It had no light. It had no sun.
It had no trees. It had no air,
No animals, or flowers fair.

God made the sun, to give us light,
The moon and stars, to shine at night.
He made the grass. He made the trees.
He made the waters and the seas.

From the dust, God man did mold.
He was lifeless, still, and cold.
Then God breathed into his nose,
"And man became a living soul."

Though other men may disbelieve,
I will not thus His Spirit grieve.
I cannot evolution crown,
Nor say that life came of its own.

Men theorize. They explore space;
But I God's word and truth embrace.
And though a host of gods abound,
Only one true God can be found.

So I believe in You, O God.
Lord, I believe in You.
And though I may be troubled sore,
Help me to trust You evermore.

Great God Who Lives Forever
Psalm 104:19

Great God who lives forever,
You have great and mighty power.
Times and seasons are in Your hand.
By You, time can move or stand.

Great God who lives forever,
You have great and mighty power;
Change the seasons?
Yes, You may.

You shorten night, and extend day.
Great God who lives forever,
You have great and mighty power;
Guiding worlds You placed in space.

You set up kings, and kings abase.
Great God who lives forever,
By Your great and mighty power,
Save frail humans by Your grace.
Let us live to see Your face.

God's Wisdom Bank
James 1:5

God's wisdom bank is like a well.
How wise God is, we never can tell.
God draws and draws from His great bank:
And lo and behold! It's a fathomless tank!

His wisdom is great; that we can tell.
He created the land, and the sea as well.
He made the stars that are up in the air,
And He created the angels fair.

Marvelous! He existed first,
Before He created the universe.
He existed before the mountains or seas,
Before the earth, the sun, or the breeze.

Then men began to use their power,
To build a great and lofty tower.
And they surely built that tower high,
Intending to build it up to the sky.

But God came down at a certain hour,
And drove the rebellious ones from the tower.
So instead of ascending, to earth they came down.
And that was the end of their fame and renown.

They thought they had protection found,
In slime for mortar, and brick for stone.
Instead of resolving to do what was right,
They thought they would God's wisdom fight.

They did not think to cease from wrong,
To worship God as they went along;
The God of heaven who sent the flood,
Who gave them strength, and wealth and food.

(continued)

God's Wisdom Bank (continued)

What lesson does this hold for all?
Tells us God is great, and we are small,
And that we should do just what He says;
For He can sustain and uphold us always.

He determines the boundaries of the sea,
But extends His love to you, and to me.
And although His throne is great and high,
To the humble of heart, He always draws nigh.

What wisdom does God have to share!
It is found around us everywhere.
It's not always with the strong or renown,
That God's great wisdom can be found.

Wisdom is heeding what we are told.
It is not in worldliness, or being bold.
One is so wise when he obeys;
In heeding what God's precepts says.

From God's great wisdom we can draw,
When we respect His will, and His law.
Come draw, and draw, without chagrin,
For it's indeed, a ceaseless spring.

God's wisdom bank is like a well.
How wise He is, we never can tell.
He draws and draws, from His great bank.
And lo and behold! It's a fathomless tank!

God's wisdom is great! Hallelujah!
God's wisdom is great!

Coping with Death

Sorrowful Lament with Hope
1 Corinthians 15:51–52

> In memory of
> my late sister,
> Loreta Priscilla Niles

Dementia is a cruel thing.
It gets between you and your kin.
Sometimes it even causes strife,
And causes ruin of one's life.

Its victims no more understand,
What basic things their lives demand.
For it steals precious memories,
And heeds not one's requests or pleas.

Lives that were cheerful, warm, and bright,
Are then subdued with no delight.
Yes, sometimes they may even smile
As if they're cheered for just a while.

When they were young, it wasn't so.
With vigor they "got up and go"
To do their tasks with willingness,
And by their deeds, others were blessed.

May God look down upon their plight,
And turn their darkness into light.
I know that one day He'll fulfill
His promises and holy will.

For He will only speak a word
That these victims will have heard—
The loving voice of Christ their King,
And they'll rejoice, and shout, and sing,

To God the everlasting One,
And to Christ, His blessed Son,
Who died that He might set them free;
They'll be restored eternally.

Peace and Resurrection
1 Thessalonians 4:13–18

Lord, help me to be ready
When my time comes to die.
Please let me be brave,
With peace, no despairing cry.

Turn the ensuing darkness
Into a temporary night.
Let me wake to Your glory,
And Your angels of light.

If I'm saved through Christ Jesus,
I'll be ready all right;
With my sins all forgiven,
Clothed in His robe so white.

At the sound of Your trumpet,
I will rise from my grave.
And sail through the air
With those who are saved.

Death Will Be Sweet Sleep
1 Corinthians 15:51–54

Death can be sweet, sweet sleep for thee.
It will be sweet, sweet sleep for me;
Knowing that I will be waking up
With Christ to spend eternity.

Oh how I love the thought of it;
Waking up by trumpet sound,
And seeing Jesus coming down,
With holy angels to escort us home.

It's not that death itself is sweet.
It's knowing that we're just asleep.
Oh death, you are forbidden to keep
God's children who have fallen asleep.

Death, you will be banished and be gone.
God's saints will then live on and on.
Thus death will be sweet sleep for me.
If I shall live eternally.

I Will See God's Lovely Face
Job 19:25–27

The face of death cannot scare me
Because I know that God is near me.
At death, I'll rest in peace, in Christ,
I will wait to hear His welcome voice;

From the grave God's saints will come forth,
Rising from east, west, south, and north.
I hope that instantly we all shall raise,
Our grateful voices, giving Him much praise.

Then I shall see the lovely face,
Of Him who saves me by His grace.
He'll hold me in His warm embrace,
And take me to the eternal heavenly place.

My Sister Rose Ann

Ephesians 6:1

Everyone who knows her knows,
Rose Ann is a fragrant rose.
And as now her life is weighed,
We saw virtues she displayed.

Trusted when on errands sent,
Trusted then to sew and mend.
Trusted then to plan and cook,
Trusted with the record book.

She was known for diligence,
Honesty, without pretense.
Father said, "Of all the rest,
She was just the very best."

He said, "She is the one to keep."
She worked so hard to sow and reap.
She made sure our family was fed,
As God provided our daily bread.

And when the time for marriage came,
Father uttered words the same.
He said if the marriage suffered lack,
He would gladly take her back.

Rose Ann, my elder sister dear,
Rest in peace, and do not fear.
I know your God looks down on you,
With smiles of love, and pity too.

And when on resurrection day,
The trumpet sounds, without delay
Jesus will take you through the skies,
To reign with Him in paradise.

Trusting God's Ability to Help and Save

By God Who Is Creator
Genesis 2:1–3

By God who is Creator, and Jesus Christ our Saviour,
The commandments are unshaken forevermore.

By God who is Creator, and Jesus Christ our Saviour.
The seventh day is the Sabbath, and no other.

By God who is Creator, and Jesus Christ our Saviour,
Salvation provides for us an open door.

God is our Creator, and Jesus Christ our Saviour.
Their arms are strong to save us forevermore.

Our Worst Enemy
1 Corinthians 15:55–56

The last enemy God destroys is death,
But sin is our worst enemy yet.
Sin affects us way beyond the grave.
Abandon sin, if you wish to be saved.

Death can take us. The grave can hold us;
But without sin, they cannot keep us.
Christ has power over death and grave,
He conquered sin so we can be saved.

I'll Praise God Whatever
Psalm 28:7

School or no school, employed or unemployed,
A million friends or friendless, light or obscurity,
I love God, and I know that He loves me.
With Him I can sail the roughest sea.

With Him I can brave the fiercest storm,
So long as I'm held by His powerful arm.
I will praise Him though my day be long,
When my work is hard, or temptation strong.

When I'm tired, discouraged, rejected or blue,
My God is reliable, strong, faithful, and true.
So sing with me now. Sing a new happy song,
For He'll guide us to heaven, deliver us from wrong.

He will protect us like no one else can,
Since he is the great and Almighty One.
He will lead us from darkness, to beams of pure light.
And this He will do by His justice and might. Praise God.

Let Me Bless the Lord
Job 2:9–19

Let me not curse God and die.
Let me not my faith deny.
Let me bless the Lord and live,
Everlastingly; to give
Praises to His name.

God Sent Light, Joy, and Peace
2 Samuel 22:29

I journeyed on through darkness drear,
Sometimes alone, I travelled there.
It seemed as if there was no end in sight;
While journeying through the darkest night.

Then, darkness fled, and light shone all around.
Joy, and peace, and gladness, instantly I found.
 Glorious light! What contrast from the past.
And not far beyond, a pure church stood at last.

Breathtaking sight; What calmness, what serenity!
One could not ask for a more heavenly place to be.
That church with steeple pointing toward the sky,
Was comfort to my heart, and feasting to my eyes.

Father, thanks for grace and bounteous love,
Which You have sent to us from heaven above.
Now with longing eyes we watch for Your return.
So come and claim the pure church as Your own.

Now sever us from sins that bind us fast,
That we may gain a heavenly home at last.
Joy shall be ours, when You take us home,
Never more in sin and darkness here to roam.

The Mighty Tug of War
Philippians 4:13

Ongoing is a mighty tug of war.
Our opponent comes to maim and mar.
He wants to wrestle us from God's hands,
But he will fail at God's supreme command.

We are no match for him in this great fight,
But we must resist in the Almighty's might.
And though we may be bruised and scarred,
Our help comes from the Lord of lords.

Through Christ the conflict will be won;
For our opponent is the conquered one.
There are things that only Christ can do.
And He can give us strength to conquer, too.

Remember Christ has died upon the cross;
So that we'll not suffer dread, defeat, or loss.
The strength we need, comes from Christ,
Call on Him then, and in His name rejoice.

Christ will win the mighty tug of war;
Then we'll rejoice in Him forevermore.
Forever blessed, Christ our Lord shall be.
For this we'll praise Him through eternity.

Christ's Victory over Satan
John 3:16–17

Have you ever heard of the war in heaven,
When victory to Christ was given?
When one of the angels of God rebelled,
And encouraged others to join him as well?

It was then that war in heaven broke out,
And the devil and his angels were cast out.
So down to earth that evil angel came,
With "great wrath" to do the very same.

On earth he successfully tempted man,
And there was where our troubles began;
But God would not abandon the beings,
Which He placed on earth without sin.

So God sent His Son to die for men,
So the devil would lose his hold on them.
Christ won in heaven, and will win henceforth;
For precious to Him are His beings on earth.

When Christ went to fast in the wilderness,
The devil came also to taunt and harass.
But Christ was filled with holy power,
Which caused the devil to flee and cower.

He wanted Christ, to turn stones into bread,
To doubt He was one with the Godhead,
To give him worship, due to God alone;
Just what he craved, coveting God's throne.

Christ conquered him in earth and heaven,
Laud and honor then to Christ was given.
And we love Him, because He rescued all,
And does deliver when on Him we call.

Gratitude
Psalm 100:4

When Jesus healed ten lepers,
He healed them all; all ten,
But none, save one poor leper,
Came thanking Him again.

When He forgave two sinners
For evils they had done,
One had thoughts of gratitude,
The other one had none.

And so the grateful sinner,
Bestowed on Him her wealth,
For she realized His goodness,
Had brought her soul good health.

And now that Jesus found me,
And took my sins away,
I now with gladness thank my Lord,
And praise Him every day.

And we should thank our Saviour,
For grace, and sins forgiven,
For life, and all the precious things,
That He to us has given.

Leave the Cleansing to God
Ephesians 2:8

Do you know that we can never begin,
To cleanse our own souls from sin?
It is God alone that can make hearts right;
And make our garments spotless and white.

I am glad that God knows just what to do,
When we call on Him to make us anew.
We repent. He then sends His Spirit like rain,
And by His baptism, we're made over again.

Sometimes we think we can change on our own,
Or sometimes we simply our errors bemoan.
And we wonder oft, about what can be done,
For sins we commit against God and His Son.

But all our worries are just in vain.
What comes of them is only more pain.
And no matter how hard we work or try,
If God does not save, we'll eternally die.

Aren't you glad that God knows what to do
About our sins and our iniquities, too?
He made the plan before we were born,
To cure our sins, by the death of His Son.

Riding on God's Train
1 Corinthians 6:9–11

The gay folks won't be gay anymore,
For they will all repent, and be pure,
And will ride on God's train
To the New Jerusalem.

The drunkards won't be lying in dirt.
They will all be wary, sober, and alert,
And will ride on God's train
To the New Jerusalem.

Swindlers won't be swindling at all.
They will be responding to God's call.
And will ride on God's train
To the New Jerusalem.

Murderers won't be murdering again.
Eagerly they'll defend God's name,
And will ride on God's train
To the New Jerusalem.

All the saved will be looking above,
A happy people filled with God's love,
And will ride on God's train
To the New Jerusalem.

It's Meant to Make You Glad
Hebrews 12:5–11

Misfortune and the cares of life
Can really make you sad.
They can keep you so depressed,
That you will scarce be glad.

They can make you really bitter.
They can rob your faith in God.
But oh, that you could only see,
They're but the "chastening rod."

So let Your nerves not shatter,
And do not grow so sad;
For though the rod is oft so sore,
It's meant to make you glad.

We Wrestle Against Evil
Ephesians 6:2

While we all prepare to sleep,
Evil angels walk the streets.
Blacker than the shades of night,
They are hidden from our sight.

Yet we know that they are there,
Spreading discord and despair.
Let us then God's armor take.
Let us watch for Jesus' sake.

They are roaming o'er the land,
And they're working hand in hand.
Let us faithful vigils keep.
We should not be caught asleep.

They'll be conquered by and by,
For our Saviour reigns on high.
With ten thousand angels bright,
He'll dispel the works of night.

God has promised strength to all
Who upon His name should call.
Then, let's watch and wary be,
Until Christ shall set us free

From this cruel and dark domain
Of the beings who cause us pain.
Father, we would live with Thee,
Throughout all eternity.

In Thee I Hope
Psalm 71:5–6

I cannot stand up or turn around.
I cannot get my feet off the ground.
I cannot work here. I cannot study there.
They are making my life a world of fear.
But I have hope.

No blood in my veins, or brains in my head?
My acquaintances think I'm as good as dead.
They think I'm as dumb, as dumb can be.
No usefulness in my life they see;
But I have hope.

Don't be glad of my misfortunes and mistakes.
And do not rejoice that I've fallen in my pace,
For God will lift me to my feet,
Then His goodness and praises I'll repeat;
For I have hope.

Some folks think that I will never excel.
Oh how they deride and condemn me as well.
But if God has blessed me, I have no fear,
That I to His glory, good fruits will bear,
For I have hope.

They are trying to take away all my hope.
I feel as if I'm tied with a rope.
But I know the Lord will have mercy on me.
He will loose my bonds, and He'll set me free.
This is my hope.

O source of hope and true wisdom,
Teach me Thyself, since I am dumb.
Cause blood to flow within my veins.
Let there be sense within my brain.
In Thee I hope.

Help me to learn. Teach me how to cope.
Be Thou my wisdom, strength, and hope.
And give me overcoming power,
To trust You daily, every hour.
In Thee I hope.

Faith and Hope
Mark 11:22

Thick, dark clouds gathered, as if to hide God's face,
But the sun shone through as a token of His grace.
As if to say, "Never fear, even now have faith."
Faith dispelled the darkness, opened heaven's gate.

At the same time there was ringing in my ear,
The sweetest song that I ever did hear.
Like a great solemn choir singing afar,
A melodious song of harmonious accord.

I am satisfied there was ringing in my ear,
Such a beautiful song, which brought joy, dispelled fear.
And behind those dark clouds, was the glowing sun.
Now new rays of faith and hope, have suddenly sprung.

Turn Aside from Suicide
Isaiah 63:9

They cannot make the grade.
They are dropping out of school.
They are under so much pressure,
Learning "great-grandfather's rule."

Some students are distressed,
So now they turn aside,
And for shame are now causing,
Their own death by suicide.

When poor grades frustrate,
And debts are mounting high;
When evil men harass you,
And even make you cry.

Turn to God, dear friends.
That is the only thing to do.
I am sure that He has better plans,
In this life for you.

Dear young men and young women,
Now do I hear you say, that you cannot
Meet your parents, and friends that way;
That you would rather commit suicide?

I think they would rather know, that you
Would only trust God to see you through,
Than to know that you are dead and gone,
And never would return home again.

And if in your fragile veins,
Some drugs you think to push,
Or down your own stomach,
Gobble poison pills and such;

(continued)

Throw away that poison now.
Please throw away that dope.
While your breath remains,
There has to be some hope.

Don't jump from that roof, don't jump.
Forget all your pride and your pomp.
Don't jump from that bridge. Don't jump.
Whoever is tempted, don't jump.

Battle for Bread?
2 Kings 6:25–29

Could it be that there would come a time,
When food would be scarce and hard to find?
Could the food situation become so bad,
That poor folks would then also grow sad?

Would mice and man have to battle for bread,
Would man have to hide food under his head?
It could be; for famine will be a last day sign,
That will come on the earth, upon mankind.

In such times we can only turn to God,
So He can supply daily our needed food.
He will surely answer if to Him we plead;
He cares, and is always aware of our needs.

Survival
Genesis 41:1–57

Once there was a time of plenty,
When the land was filled with food.
Not one bowl or plate was empty.
Times were very, very good.

Pharaoh knew what was brewing.
Joseph made him understand
That a famine would be coming
On the fair and pleasant land.

So they built large storehouses,
For to keep their surplus corn.
And they laid up all the fatness,
As they worked hard, everyone.

Then came the time of famine,
When the east wind blasted all.
But the people did not famish,
Careful planning saved them all.

And not one of them did perish,
For the coming evil was foretold.
God saved the land through Joseph,
They survived by the corn he sold.

Kind versus Unkind Employers
Philippians 4:19

"We have no jobs. We will not hire."
These words I would often hear
From those behind their desks.
Such replies were hard to bear.

Let me stop and think for a moment.
Something might be wrong, I guess.
Seems I'm robbed of life's contentment,
But onward, with new courage I'll press.

I thought of my former employers,
And knew that not all were kind.
Though some of them were pleasant,
There were some who boggled my mind.

With sadness I roamed the city,
To see what jobs I could find.
But none showed kindness or pity.
Could it be for faults left behind?

I'm outspoken and have an accent.
I wondered what else was not right.
My garments aren't laces or ruffles.
There's nothing to dazzle their sight.

But at last! I found an employer
Who seemed to forgive my past;
And kindly without much prying,
This one gave me a job at last!

She ignored outward appearance.
And before I could scarcely realize,
I was on the job and working.
'Twas as if I had found a great prize.

My friends, what would poor people do
Without kind employers who are so few,
Whom I think God has used in His employ,
To hire the rejected and the unemployed?

Just so, if your past was sinful,
And you know you're bound for hell.
Come to Christ, that kind forgiver,
He'll erase your sins as well.

God Will Sustain
Isaiah 58:11

In the time of drought or famine,
Whether you are young or old,
If the God of heaven is with you,
He will surely satisfy your soul.

Cold Chasing Song and Prayer
James 5:13–16

One day Mother dear arose,
To find one child with stuffy nose;
With trouble breathing out and in,
And one child had goose-pimpled skin.

And so not knowing what to do,
Mother thought a while, got a cue;
And then it was not very long,
Ere she made up a cold-chasing song.

"Someday, someday this cold weather will pass away.
Someday, someday, this cold weather will pass away.
We'll be going over yonder to that pleasant shore,
There we'll not experience cold weather anymore.

Someday, someday, this cold weather will pass away.
Someday, someday, this cold weather will pass away.
For God will give us stable and pleasant temperature.
And we'll not experience cold weather anymore."

"In the meantime, let us begin to pray.
Heavenly Father, holy is Thy name.
We thank You for sparing our lives thus far.
We pray that You will keep us in Your care,
And chase the cold away.
In Jesus' name we pray."

Experiencing God's Love

Morning Wish
Matthew 6:9

Lord, I feel Your love this morning
As I wake up from my sleep.
I know You're the loving Father
That doth all Your children keep.

Now let Your radiant sunshine
And Your free redeeming grace,
Invigorate my dull senses,
As I gaze upon Your face.

May this day be filled with blessings,
And whatever comes my way,
Be it pain or disappointment,
May it be a glorious day.

Glad and Grateful
1 John 1:9

God does not badger me about my flaws;
He just covers them, and that's because
He knows I willingly repent,
That heavenward my heart is bent.

He knows my weaknesses and fears,
And He has dried my many tears.
He calls me when I go astray,
And leads me to the "narrow way."

What precious, overwhelming love
That comes to me from heaven above.
I'm grateful for His loving care;
May it go with me everywhere.

What We Need Most
Ephesians 4:7–8

We all have gifts, but we all need love.
Obtained, we shall praise our God above.
Then we'll live in harmony, joy, and peace,
And our happiness will never cease.

Teach Us How to Love
Ephesians 4:32

Father, teach us how to love
Mortals on earth and Thee above.
To love those who cause us sore distress,
And those who bring us happiness.

To love the pleasant, and the mean;
The lowly peasant, king, or queen.
We find it hard to truly love,
Mortals on earth, as Thee above.

We know not how to love at all.
We know though, how to build a wall
To keep all pain and sorrow out,
Which cause us oft to fret and doubt.

So change us now, that we may know,
Just how to love our foes below.
That You may give us perfect love,
To love mankind and Thee above.

God Loves You
John 15:9–12

Know that God loves you,
Though others may despise you.
And do not fret though you're despised,
For those who hate, do not realize,

God loves good men, and sinners too.
If they knew that, they would love you.
So rest content. In time they'll know,
God upon all, His love bestows.

And pray that somehow they will find,
That to all, God is loving, good, and kind.

Salvation Through Christ and Other Vital Truths

Figurative Mountain
Isaiah 1:18

There is a white mountain,
Above a dark valley below.
It is bright and shining.
It is as white as snow.

It is not whitened by paint,
And not whitened by snow;
But by God's righteousness.
There is the place to go.

It towers o'er the darkness
Of the woe and sin below.
If you are lost in sin, my friends,
It's there that you must go.

The road that leads to the top,
Is also white as snow.
You must stay upon that road;
The one safe way to go.

And that road is narrow,
Leading onward and up.
Yield not to vain distractions,
As you strive to reach the top.

There is naught at the bottom,
Save sorrow, strife, and fear;
Also broad confusing roads,
Are found beneath it there.

Christ is more than willing,
To make your sins like snow.
If you are lost in sin, my friends,
It's to Him you must go.

Christ Is Our Righteousness
Philippians 3:6–9

I awoke one restful morning,
With joy within my heart.
For God had sent His blessing,
A brand-new day to start.

And oh, that blessed morning
I had something on my mind.
It is a precious treasure,
I wish that all could find.

It was not thoughts of pleasure,
Of silver nor of gold;
And of this pleasant treasure,
The half has not been told.

It was the Spirit speaking,
Blessed assurance to my soul;
That Christ is our righteousness.
What good news to my soul!

Christ is our righteousness!
By this we're very blessed.
"To Him shall every mortal bow,
And every tongue confess."

Christ is our righteousness!
That was the treasure dear,
Which I found that morning.
To keep it is my prayer.

A treasure of all treasures!
The one I hold most dear.
I find no other treasure,
To this one can compare.

Listen World—God's Love Song to You
1 John 5:19

Dearest World:

You are not just randomly floating in space.
You are the object of My love and grace.

And since you are the object of My love,
I've come to woo you to My home above.

Listen world. Listen world. Listen world.
Listen world. Listen world. Listen world.

You are Mine, though you were deceived.
Who came before were robbers, and thieves.

Despising My commandments and My laws,
Their coming was self-interest, not My cause.

Listen world. Listen world. Listen world.
Listen world. Listen world. Listen world.

I sent My servants time and time again
With messages you may not comprehend.

Now I Myself am reaching out to you,
So you'll realize My love for you is true.

Listen world. Listen world. Listen world.
Listen world. Listen world. Listen world.

Listen World—God's Love Song to You (continued)

Will you listen to My earnest loving call?
What more can I do but give you My all?

I sent My only Son to die for you,
So you'll have endless life, and riches, too.

Listen world. Listen world. Listen world.
Listen world. Listen world. Listen world.

Soon He'll be coming back to you again.
So little time for you to act remains.

Will you accept My pleadings of true love;
And come to dwell within my house above?

Listen world. Listen world. Listen world.
Listen world. Listen world. Listen world.

Whom Shall I Choose?
Matthew 10:32–39

The question is, whom shall I choose,
When it comes to choosing sides?
Would I choose my friends instead of Christ?
If I point them to Christ, I might lose them,
For they may not want to learn about Him.
They may prefer to cling to their sins.

Though my friends are so precious to me,
I should help them the love of Christ to see.
And let them know that He died for their sin.
That a brand-new life, He wants them to begin.
But that it requires, their faith and their love,
To become part of His kingdom above.

Would they begin to hate me all they could,
If I tell them of the things that I should?
Would they be angry, if I tell them of Christ,
Of the way to heaven, and eternal life?
I must forget the pain that I must suffer.
Even my life, I should not consider,

If I choose to tell my friends about Christ,
Will they repent and in Him rejoice?
If they reject Christ, What more can I do?
He wants me to tell them news that is true,
And that they're invited to come to Him, too,
So that their hearts He will gladly renew.
Hard choice; but I made the choice
To choose God, and give up my friends.

Right choice, painful choice,
But joyous choice in the end.
And I hope that in choosing Christ,
And giving up my earthly friends,
That I will be happy with God and Christ,
And will find my dear friends in the end.

Followed
Hebrews 13:5

The church is a part of our lives,
And it was meant to be;
So never, never, never,
Seek from its courts to flee.

I fled from the church in my sorrow,
Thinking the church no more I would see.
Through the woods alone I headed,
But God was present with me.

The church seemed far in the distance,
As I left it behind my back,
But God still followed with patience,
And a clear stream rose in my track.

I was far from the church and the people,
Who gathered to worship within,
But that stream the church reflected,
And I saw its image therein,

My heart was filled with wonder.
I was overwhelmed with awe,
When I gazed at the church in the distance,
And realized 'twas the same that I saw.

"The church is too far, too far," I said,
To be mirrored in this clear stream."
But it was true, that very church,
Was still the church of my dream.

Now I hope I'll see Jesus forever,
Who died for the church and for me.
Then there shall be no parting ever,
Between that dear church and me.

The Perfect Pastor
Jeremiah 23:1–4

Jesus is the perfect pastor,
That can counter all disasters.
Tenderly He tends His flock.
All the lost He will bring back.

Keeps them in His loving arms,
So they will not suffer harm.
In the safety of His fold,
He protects from heat and cold.

Tender Shepherd, All in All;
Watching so they would not fall.
Gives them joy and peace within,
And the grace to conquer sin.

Joyfully they sing His praise.
Of His kindness they're amazed.
Nevermore will they be moved;
For they're thankful for His love.

Be on Guard, Watchmen
Ephesians 8:10–18

Watchmen, you must blow the trumpet.
Watchmen, you must sound the alarm.
God watches over His people;
He wants to protect them from harm.

God places you in a position,
To see the approaching storm.
To herd His people to safety,
Until it is tranquil and calm.

As through a giant telescope,
You will see the enemy afar,
Who comes with hate and enmity,
To rage a destructive war.

You must see the enemy approaching.
Who is as fierce as a raging storm.
You know his defeat will be certain,
For Christ has spoken his doom.

It is not by their might or power,
That the saints will engage in the fight;
For it is only through God's Spirit,
That they can defend the right.

Neither betrayers or traitors,
Can help the enemy to win;
Then, just let the Holy Spirit
Quell disloyalty and sin.

Then all God's loyal soldiers
Will honor their rightful King,
Who from eternal ages,
Gave His life that the church may win.

Watchmen, you must blow the trumpet.
Watchmen, you must sound the alarm.
So all may put on God's armor,
To protect them from sin's deadly harm.

Sensible versus Silly Soldiers
2 Timothy 2:3–5

All the soldiers' chance had come,
To fight with all their might.
With strategic operations,
They sought to win the fight.

They were as busy as could be,
And they worked so willingly.
Seems as if they were all content,
And never an idle moment spent.

But one soldier left his employ,
Just to play with a small child's toy.
He acted as though he had full release,
And as if the raging war had ceased.

And it could be clearly seen,
That more help was coming in.
But the silly soldier was not keen,
And ignored the help which came then.

So with spiritual battles in this life,
There are soldiers unwise and inept.
But some equipped to quell the strife,
Act with sense, and are very adept.

The Bell with the Clapper
1 Corinthians 14:8

Back and forth, forth and back.
That old bell has lost its knack.
South to north, back and forth;
All it does is rock, and rock.

What's the matter with that bell?
Rocking it does very well,
But not a single chime would swell;
And so the time it cannot tell.

The clapper of that bell is gone,
So it can neither rouse nor warn.
A lesson in that bell I see,
That clearly speaks to you and me.

Just so, without God's Spirit,
We can't do anything.
And if we ever do some good,
We owe it all to Him.

But then another bell I hear.
With sound distinct, chime so clear.
In contrast to that useless bell,
It has a message it can tell.

You can know when night is coming.
You may know of approaching dawn.
You will know when noon is nearing.
Clearly, you'll know when it is morn.

The bell is in tune with its master.
Its clapper is sound and intact.
Its sound is with timely precision.
Each soul can feel its impact.

Like the good bell with the clapper,
Whose message is distinct and clear,
Let us tell of our long-looked-for Saviour,
Let us tell that His coming is near.

God's Clocks
Acts 2:19–21

I hear several loud tick tocks,
Coming from God's mighty clocks.
God made the sun and moon to shine.
They're also made to tell the time.

Christ said that the stars would fall.
And this was meant to speak to all;
To say that He will come again,
And everlastingly will reign.

The falling stars? They mark off time;
Like sun and moon, when they with earth align.
They are telling us that little time remains,
When God shall send His Son to earth again.

Such warning signs aren't limited to stars.
They're also manifested in endless wars;
In famines and in numerous earthquakes,
In tribulation, and in pestilence.

But if we're deaf, we surely will not hear,
And we'll ignore them if we do not care.
But God's great clocks will never cease to chime,
Telling us that Christ will come again on time.

Peace When? and Where?
1 Thessalonians 5:1–3

Of men of love, there are but few.
And we all know that this is true.
And so, because they lack true love,
They with wars their problems solve.

Here in this world we hear men say,
That peace has come, and here to stay.
But in this world there is no peace,
Not in the West nor in the East.

If to God's Word we would take heed,
In His great Book we there will read,
When peace and safety men doth cry,
Sudden destruction is then nigh.

In that good land that God shall give,
In peace and safety we shall live.
There will be no need to war or fight,
For Christ our King will do what's right.

In that fair land yes, peace shall flow,
And everlastingly, we'll know
That only Christ can give true peace,
When He shall cause all wars to cease.

God's Truth Will Triumph
James 1:12

Though men may seek to hinder God's plan,
To stamp out the truth, sever its right hand,
The truth of God shall never die,
For God still lives and reigns on high.

Though darkness gather all around,
Or men of fame doth cast it down;
Though Christians' blood soaks the ground,
God's truth will triumph and abound.

Though evil men shed saints' blood,
The truth will prevail, like a flood,
And rise to heights and soar above,
To touch the dwelling place of love.

Then will God see, and will come down,
His faithful children all to crown.
Then will all find, both great and small,
That God's truth triumphs over all.

Oh, Jesus, Oh
2 Kings 2:11–12

Oh, Enoch, oh. Oh, Enoch, oh.
You kept close to God on this earth below,
And this was because you loved Him so.
Your Heavenly Father knows just why
He took you home where you'll never die.
Oh, Enoch, oh. Oh, Enoch, oh.

Oh, Elijah, oh. Oh, Elijah, oh.
Elijah prayed and it did not rain;
Then He prayed, and rain came down again.
God sent His chariot down from the sky.
It came and took you to His home on high.
Oh, Elijah, oh. Oh, Elijah, oh.

Oh, Jesus, oh. You love us so.
You came down from Your home on high,
That on the cross for us You may die.
You promised You'll come back by and by,
To take us to Your home in the sky.
Oh, Jesus, oh. Oh, Jesus, oh.

God's Forgiveness
Colossians 1:19–20

God made a very perfect world,
And placed a man therein;
And then He placed a woman there,
But neither one had sin.

He blessed the man with wisdom,
To name some things He made:
The birds and quiet animals,
And not one was afraid.

The man He made was Adam.
The woman's name was Eve.
Their home was oh, so happy!
They had no cause to grieve.

Their home was decked with flowers,
Included were fruit-bearing trees.
Their visitor was God Himself.
And they were very pleased.

But one day Eve went roaming,
And Adam knew it not;
Came back with a forbidden thing,
A strange fruit that she got.

God warned the fruit was harmful,
To eat it death would come.
But she was not so careful.
She ate and brought some home.

Although the fruit looked harmless,
It would cause them both to die.
Alone they would not suffer,
But so would you and I.

(continued)

God's Forgiveness (continued)

Both she and Adam ate it.
How much they disobeyed!
It made God so unhappy,
And they were so afraid.

By the devil they were tempted,
Their God to disobey.
Yielding, sin came and spoiled their joy
And took their home away.

But God forgave them gladly,
And sent His Son to die;
That Adam, Eve, and all His saints,
Can live with Him on high.

What God Requires of Us

Glory to My King

Isaiah 12:5–6

Zion's songs I sweetly sing;
Glory, glory to my King.
Zion's joys I have untold;
Zion's sights I now behold.

Fellowshipping with my King,
Why should I not praise and sing,
For the joys He gives to me,
For His grace which sets me free?

I will always sing His praise,
All throughout my pilgrim days;
Till He comes and takes me home,
Nevermore on earth to roam.

Focusing on God
Psalm 89:15–16

As the sunflower turns to the sun,
So let me turn to You, O God;
To behold Your power and might.

Just to feel Your warmest love,
Coming from Your throne above.
May I walk in Your pure light,
Though You're hidden from my sight.

While awaiting Christ's new dawn,
Of Your Spirit, let me be born.
Let me pattern You each day.
Let me be Yours forever, I pray.

Your Body Is My Temple
1 Corinthians 6:19–20

"Your body is My temple,
Dwelling of the Divine.
For My glory I have made you;
You are wholly Mine.

It's use is not for you
Or other mortals to decide.
For I Am your only Wisdom,
Your Counsellor and guide.

You are not made to house
Foul spirits, of murder or of hate.
You are not made for fornication,
Contention or debate.

Covetousness and envy,
Must not be found within.
Boasting, pride, or deceit,
Or other grievous sins.

You are made for deeds of goodness,
God's law within your heart.
In light of coming judgment,
Is reason to repent.

And for this very reason,
My Spirit I have sent,
That for My free salvation,
You now may thus repent."

—God

Jesus, Shine Your Light on Me
Psalm 51:1–2, 15

Jesus, shine Your light on me,
Now and through eternity.
All Your goodness to proclaim,
So that all may praise Your name.

I Worship the God of Heaven
Revelation 14:7

I worship God who made the sun,
And all the host of heaven.
But never will I worship gods
Which mortal hands have graven.

I worship God who made the world,
And all the things therein,
Instead of worshipping false gods,
I give the praise to Him.

Read the Bible, Friends
2 Timothy 3:15–16

Do not take what others said,
Though the Bible they have read.
You should read the Bible, too.
Try to read it through and through.

It tells of God the Father,
And Christ the Holy One,
Who is the world's Redeemer,
And God's beloved Son.

I read the Bible all the time.
It's healing to my heart and mind.
The troubles in the world today,
Demand we read it while we pray.

It can be our stronghold,
And our protective tower.
From it we can get courage,
And overcoming power.

Power to do what is right,
And resist the wrong,
The power of salvation;
It can make us strong.

It is God's healing water;
Not intoxicating wine.
It can be a banquet.
Come and freely dine.

And after we have read it,
It should soften our hearts.
Of our total life and actions,
It should be a vital part.

Read the Bible, Friends (continued)

Many, many read it,
But they read it all in vain,
For they stifle their convictions,
And the old man they retain.

But with true conviction,
And with willingness, we'll find,
That the Spirit will illuminate,
And clear our darkened minds.

For thus it was intended,
A light to guide our way;
To lead us to the Saviour,
"The Life, the Truth, the Way."

Disbelief and Disobedience
Genesis 13:13

The height of disbelief these days
Is surely quite alarming.
Is this the time to scorn rebuke?
Is there time left for scorning?

Be not like folks of Sodom's days,
Or those who scorned Noah's warning.
They walked in their own willful ways,
With disbelief and scorning.

Did they think that the world would never end?
That God would never His precepts defend?
Nor from heaven fires would fall
On the plains, and destroy them all?

To abnormal pleasures and sin they clung.
They grew more bold in doing wrong.
So angels came to town one night,
And told just Lot to take his flight.

Ignoring graces God had given,
Sodom's sins had reached to heaven.
They tried God's angels to abuse,
So they were blinded and confused.

We know that judgment happened before,
When Noah entered the ark, and God shut the door.
Then the rain in torrents came pouring down,
Until all the wicked people were drowned.

All that God made were "very good."
That man was pure, is understood.
Man was upright in his ways,
Before he sinned or disobeyed.

Sin entered here and took its toll.
It devastated men's poor souls.
But we are not left without hope,
In darkness to forever grope.

Disbelief and Disobedience (continued)

God gave His Son, so we would not die.
And that is just the reason why
We should take heed today,
And accept His gift without delay.

The time has come to look above,
To God who made us all.
'Tis time for us to grasp that love,
And cherish most of all,

The things unseen, yet which exist
Beyond the clouds above.
The things restored by Jesus Christ,
And bought by His own blood.

My friends, "Behold, the Lamb of God"
Who takes our sins away.
Who purchased us by His own blood,
Sustains us day by day.

He calls, and warns, and pleads,
By His servants through the ages.
He keeps on calling even now.
Why work for sin's dread wages?

Why live a life of pleasure now
To wake to pangs of pain?
He who will die to sin's lust now,
Will surely live again.

I hope You'll gladly heed God's call.
I hope the light you'll see.
Do not reject His loving call.
Obedient you should be.

Turn to your loving Lord today.
Pour out your soul to Him and say,
"Once and for all, I heed Your call.
I give you body, soul, and all."

Blow the Trumpet, Watchman
Isaiah 58:1

See the watchman yonder stands.
He stands with trumpet in his hands.
Why the trumpet is not blown,
Though the King approaches home?

Blow the trumpet, haste to blow;
So the waiting saints may know,
That it's time to be on guard,
To stand, to fight, to be prepared.

They need to hear the trumpet blow.
They need to know which way to go.
For they are distracted sore,
While their King is at the door.

Blow the trumpet for the wise.
They would not want to be surprised.
Blow the trumpet for the strong.
They want to know they are not wrong.

Blow the trumpet, watchman.
Blow! It is God who bids you to.
For His Son will come to reign,
Never to depart again.

Abiding in Christ
John 15:4–8

I want to stay in Christ always;
Like Him to live, like Him to pray.
Some losses I shall then sustain,
But then, eternity I'll gain.

Words of kindness I must sow;
Deeds of love I must bestow.
Comfort give to sick and dying,
Always on His strength relying.

Close to those who suffer pain,
Doing naught for selfish gain.
Those oppressed, to set them free.
Christ has done the same for me.

Mutual Concern
Mark 6:7, 12

Now is the time for sharing and caring.
A time for concern for the erring.
For caring for friends whatever the cost.
A time to seek for those who are lost.

In life, we need God's help in all we do.
But we need to work in unison, too.
Moving in unison, more can be done
Than what is accomplished one by one.

We may be weary as we travel along,
But we are ordered to get things done.
And since God has given us the might.
Let us do all we can to win the fight.

So trust in God. Be not overwhelmed,
And we will win with Christ at the helm.
And knowing our strength cannot be enough,
Let's trust in God when the going is rough.

Let's give Him praise while in the fight,
For the outcome will be glorious alright,
Since we're battling for the right,
In Jehovah's strength and might.

To Share with Love
Proverbs 4:21

I saw an old and careworn face,
Encased within a frame.
I could not help but notice it,
And gazed upon the same.

The picture that I briefly saw,
Mirrored this face of mine.
But it was oh, so awful,
I could not stand the sight.

Displeased with such an image,
I hacked at it with all my might,
To find a better visage,
To see a better sight.

But as I chipped away my face,
Other sights were frightening to see.
It was a scene most horrible;
Dreadful scenes of poverty.

Unkempt, barefooted children,
Were peering out at me.
All motionless they stood there,
And as helpless as could be.

My picture I thought was horrible;
Now what is this I must see?
Poor children in a log-sided house,
With a grass roof, was shown to me.

I could not stand the sight of it.
What scenes of poverty.
I thought my picture was so bad,
Not fit at all to see.

(continued)

To Share with Love (continued)

But now I see that there are those,
In conditions more horrible than I.
If I should gaze a moment more,
That scene could make me cry.

Came morning, and so I went to the mall,
Where I viewed the people, one and all.
They were walking around and richly clad.
And sure I thought my condition was bad.

For my boots were old, and they were torn,
And my coat was whole, but it was worn.
The hat on my head was far from being new.
The rest of my clothes were neat but old, too.

When I came home, I looked at our floor,
As the sun shone through the big glass door.
It reflected on a clean carpet of gold.
That was new. It was not at all old.

The furniture was neat, And also lovely.
Then the scenes of the past night,
Came back clearly to me:

Of the people's grass house
That was far from neat,
And their scanty old clothes,
And no shoes on their feet.

As I thought upon them,
For their sake I was sad.
And now my picture,
Was not at all bad.

(continued)

To Share with Love (continued)

And so it is, for real in this life,
When some think they are poor.
They do not know, nor yet realize,
That there are millions more.

Yes, millions and millions more,
Who are living in shameful poverty,
And eating things they could not stand
Or sleeping where they would not want to be.
And so may I appreciate,
The things God gives to me.

And share with those of lesser fate,
And experiencing gross poverty.
But I must share with willingness.
Must share with joy and love.
For only thus, that I could please,
My Father in heaven above.

Beware, Beware
Jude 7

Beware, beware,
Lest we God's judgment share.

Cease from homosexuality.
Cease from adultery.
Cease from fornication.
Cease from all abomination.

Beware, beware,
Lest we God's judgment share.

Timothy
Acts 16:1–5

Timothy, young helper of Paul,
Was obedient to God's call.

He was loyal, faithful, meek,
Teaching others Christ to seek.

God, the Center of Church and Home
Isaiah 54:13

God is the center of this dear little church,
And this church is the center of our home.
The Bible is the center of this dear little church,
And this church is the center of our home.

The gospel is the center of this dear little church,
And this church is the center of our home.
God's will is the center of this dear little church,
And this church is the center of our home.

Jesus is the center of this dear little church,
And this church is the center of our home.
Heaven is the center of this dear little church,
And this church is the center of our home.

When God is the center of the church,
And the Bible is the center of the church,
And the gospel is the center of the church,
And God's will is the center of the church,

And if Jesus is the center of the church,
And heaven is the center of the church,
Then the church will be a blessed place,
To serve and bless the human race.

Noah and the Animals Obeyed
Genesis 6:8–22

God talked to Noah. Told Him to build an ark,
With a great big door, to hold people and more.
Noah listened, then did what he had to do.
What a very good example for me and for you.

Noah cut down some trees. He needed much wood
To build a strong ark to hold people and food.
He made it with rooms to hold animals, too.
I am glad that Noah did what God said to do.

Noah told all the people of the flood that would come,
But they did not want to part with their homes,
And men grew more wicked, their sins were so great,
Yet God wanted to save them from an upcoming fate.

But Noah got ready with all of his kin,
And went in the ark; then God locked them in.
And so when it rained, and the flood was high,
The ark kept them safe, so they did not die.

God had talked to the animals He had made.
They knew His voice and quickly obeyed.
They marched in order by sevens and by twos.
They were so happy to do what they should.

Some of the animals just to name a few,
Which came marching. They were saved too.
There were cattle, goats, sheep, and deer,
 Elephants, donkeys, horses, and bears.

Noah and the Animals Obeyed (continued)

There were flying fowls, and creatures that leap.
Both great and small animals, Noah had to keep.
I wish all the people then, had obeyed God, too.
If you were there, what would you do?

All the sea creatures also listened and obeyed,
They stayed in the water and were not afraid.
Water covered the earth when it rained,
But when the rain stopped it was dry again.

Suppose the animals had not obeyed,
And out in the forest they had stayed?
When all that rain from the flood came down,
All those animals would have been drowned.

The lesson to learn is that we should obey,
And listen and do whatever God says.
And instead of an ark to sail through a flood,
We will have the angels to take us to God.

And Jesus Himself will come, and you will see
That He will be smiling, and as happy as can be.
And we all will be with Him day after day
Because in His kingdom, we forever will stay.

I Want to Be like Jesus Most of All
Daniel 1:19–20

When I read within the Bible,
And learn how good men were able
To do great and mighty works for God,
When long ago this earth they trod;

It makes me want to do the same;
To give glory to God's name,
By things that God can help me do.
Both in deed and holy conduct too.

Yes, such longings come within.
I just long to respond and to begin,
If Christ Himself would upon me call,
And turns me around as He did to Paul.

I want to be like those good men.
I'm hoping God would use me like them;
Just as He used Stephen, or used Paul.
And I want to be like Jesus most of all.

To me Jesus is the best of them all.
And although that I would even
Want to be like Paul or Stephen,
I would rather be like Jesus most of all.

TEACH Services, Inc.
PUBLISHING

We invite you to view the complete
selection of titles we publish at:
www.TEACHServices.com

We encourage you to write us
with your thoughts about this,
or any other book we publish at:
info@TEACHServices.com

TEACH Services' titles may be purchased in
bulk quantities for educational, fund-raising,
business, or promotional use.
bulksales@TEACHServices.com

Finally, if you are interested in seeing
your own book in print, please contact us at:
publishing@TEACHServices.com

We are happy to review your manuscript at no charge.

www.ingramcontent.com/pod-product-compliance
Lightning Source LLC
Chambersburg PA
CBHW050847240426
43667CB00022B/2949